HEALTHFUL WAYS
REVISED

TODAY'S HEALTH

W. W. CHARTERS, PH.D.
DIRECTOR, THE RESEARCH SERVICE, STEPHENS COLLEGE, COLUMBIA, MISSOURI

DEAN F. SMILEY, M.D.
CONSULTANT IN HEALTH AND PHYSICAL FITNESS, AMERICAN MEDICAL ASSOCIATION

RUTH M. STRANG, PH.D.
PROFESSOR OF EDUCATION, TEACHERS COLLEGE, COLUMBIA UNIVERSITY

ILLUSTRATIONS EDITED BY BYRON MUSSER, INC., NEW YORK
POSED PHOTOGRAPHS BY JAMES SNYDER

AND GROWTH SERIES

*St. Peters School
Huron, Ohio*

Healthful Ways

REVISED

THE MACMILLAN COMPANY · NEW YORK

COPYRIGHT, 1941, 1947,
BY THE MACMILLAN COMPANY

All rights reserved—no part of this book may be reproduced in any form without permission in writing from the publisher, except by a reviewer who wishes to quote brief passages in connection with a review written for inclusion in magazine or newspaper.

Published January, 1941.
Revised Edition published 1947.
Seventh Printing, 1952.

TYPOGRAPHY AND DESIGN BY I. N. STEINBERG

Printed in the United States of America

FOREWORD TO THE TEACHER

In the days when subjects followed conventional patterns it was an easy matter to write textbooks. The authors attempted to make the content as simple as they could and expected the children to master what was set before them. But the subject matter itself was completely prescribed by the specialists who worked in the field.

More recently the problems of textbook authors have greatly increased in complexity. Accepting the current theory of education that the content of textbooks and courses of study should be based upon the needs and interests of children, they must radically change the old conventional subject matter. Consideration has been given to what the children need, in what grades it will be of the most interest to children, how the information can be translated into habits, the degree of difficulty of the vocabulary, and a score of other considerations.

Consequently in the preparation of the *Health and Growth Series,* of which the present books are a revision, exhaustive basic studies of a wide variety were carried on over an extended period of time:

Statistics concerning the incidence of children's diseases and accidents were collected and interpreted to provide an indication of the school age at which materials upon these subjects should be most appropriately taught. Health columns in newspapers and health bulletins for laymen were analyzed to discover the vocabulary children should be taught to enable them to continue to read intelligently popular health articles after graduation and in adult life. The difficulty of words was ascertained for each grade to enable the authors to use words known by eighty per cent of the class, except necessary technical terms, which would be carefully explained.

The initial purpose of this series is to interest the child in living healthfully. The primary method of creating this interest is to teach a unit when the learner sees a good reason for its introduction—precautions when colds

v

are in season, safety in the "accident years" of childhood. Supplementary methods are legion. They include of course illustrations that depict real health situations.

A second objective is to establish specific, flexible habits of healthful living. What one *does* is of more importance than what one *knows*. Good health is maintained by actions and not by knowledge alone. To acquire flexible habits of right living, no time is so opportune as the period of childhood. All methods of habit building should be used—interest in the activity, an understanding of its physiological purpose, repetition until essential daily routines are established, use in varied situations, and satisfaction in the outcome. The mental hygiene and the social aspects are given special emphasis.

A third objective of major importance is to furnish the child with the latest scientific information about health and disease. Much misinformation is still prevalent in the homes of the nation. This can be eradicated in the next generation only provided that the child learns proved facts in the schoolroom. Much can be eradicated in the homes of this generation by the practice of having the child read his texts with his parents.

In preparing the first thoroughly revised and completely reorganized edition, the *New Health and Growth Series,* the authors considered the health subjects for which there was increasing need in our schools. Believing that the interest in safety education should be utilized and that the subject should be taught in the elementary school grades as units in many courses at appropriate points rather than in added independent courses, the authors included a generous amount of information about the methods of assuring safety as related to health in the prevention of accidents and about the reasonableness of the rules that were presented.

In sympathy with the attention that was belatedly being given conservation and consumer education by the schools and believing, as in the case of safety education, that these desirable fields should be treated in the elementary grades as units of already existing courses, the authors devoted substantial space to conservation as applied to health and endeavored to teach the children to become skillful in getting the best for their money and their effort in matters of health and its accessories—food, clothing, vacations, recreations, medicines.

During war years, health knowledge advances rapidly. This was true in World War II. Especially in the fields of nutrition and disease prevention and control, important discoveries were made. Among these were the newer knowledge of the vitamins, the sulfa drugs, the medicinal molds—penicillin and streptomycin—and DDT and related preparations for combating insect pests. These subjects and other recently reported knowledge regarding health have been incorporated in *Today's Health and Growth Series*. In the present revision improvements have also been made along these lines: (1) the organization of content, (2) the further simplification of vocabulary and sentence structure, (3) the emphasis on the most pressing postwar health needs and on the solution of local health problems, and (4) the recognition of social and vocational motives for healthful living and the importance of each pupil's taking more responsibility for his own health and for the health of others.

The authors are indebted to many sources for the materials which they examined in their search for scientific and practical materials. Particularly they acknowledge the use of data from the writings of the National Safety Council, the American Red Cross, and the study of accidents of school children made by Miss Jeanie M. Pinckney, Chief of the Bureau of Nutrition and Health Education, Division of Extension, University of Texas. Special acknowledgment is made to Mrs. Helene Searcy Puls for her valuable assistance with the third to the eighth books, inclusive, and to Miss Leslie Hunt and Mrs. George MacLeod for their contributions to the ninth book in the series.

The illustrations, many of which were specially posed for this series, represent photography in its most modern aspect. Acknowledgment is due for specific photographs to the following: Atlas Photos, page 82; Black Star, page 66; Free Lance Photographers, pages 149 and 160; Ewing Galloway, pages 1, 2, 16, 65, 111, and 154; Massachusetts Institute of Technology, Department of Biology and Health, pages 5 and 6; R. I. Nesmith and Associates, pages 135 and 187; Paul Parker, pages 48, 73, and 230; Pix, pages 63 and 221; H. Armstrong Roberts, pages 19, 23, 41, 47, 136, 142, 143, and 177; Snyder from Monkmeyer Press Photo Service, page 94; Underwood and Underwood, page 93; U. S. Army Medical Museum, pages 100 and 125; and Welch Allyn Company, page 85. For the use of facilities supplied for the photographs acknowledgment is due also to Bausch & Lomb Optical Company; Essex House, New York City; Arthur Kudner, Inc. (Florida Citrus Commission and General Motors Corporation); F. A. O. Schwarz, New York City; S. S. White Dental Manufacturing Company; and Adolph Zukor Estate, New York City.

THE AUTHORS

CONTENTS

Unit I. How to Have Fewer Colds — 1
   COLDS SPOIL THE FUN — 3
   GERMS THAT CAUSE COLDS — 4
   HOW COLDS ARE SPREAD — 4
   WAYS TO PREVENT AND CURE COLDS — 7

Unit II. New Ways for Old — 15
   HOW SALLY CHANGED — 17
   WHO'S AFRAID — 25
   WHEN YOU MAKE A MISTAKE — 35
   WHO'S POPULAR — 41

Unit III. Healthful Days — 47
   HOW TO FIND TIME TO DO THE THINGS YOU WANT TO DO — 49
   HOW TO BE FIT FOR WORK AND PLAY — 52
   HOW TO HAVE STRENGTH TO WORK AND PLAY — 62

Unit IV. Health Tests — 73
   THE GROWING TEST — 75
   THE DOCTOR'S TESTS — 83

Unit V. More Ways to Keep Well — 93
   VISITING THE DENTIST — 95
   PREVENTING DISEASE — 103

Unit VI. On Parade — 111
   GOOD POSTURE IN SITTING AND STANDING — 113
   FEET ON PARADE — 121
   IN TRAINING — 130

UNIT VII. Food Problems   135
   VEGETABLES   137
   EGGS ALL THE YEAR AROUND   144
   SAFE MILK   147
   MINERALS AND VITAMINS   149
   PLANNING MEALS   152

UNIT VIII. Making a Better Community   159
   AN INDIAN PUEBLO   161
   HELPING YOUR COMMUNITY   161
   COMMUNITY SPIRIT   168
   KNOWING YOUR COMMUNITY   170
   SCHOOL SPIRIT   175
   HEALTH SPIRIT   179

UNIT IX. Accidents Need Not Happen   187
   THE FIRST-AID CUPBOARD   189
   SAFETY ON THE STREET AND ROAD   196
   SAFE OUTDOOR PLAY   201
   SAFETY IN SCHOOL   206
   SAFETY IN THE HOME   208

UNIT X. A Happy Vacation   221
   ACCIDENTS ON VACATION   223
   POISON IVY AND POISON SUMAC   225
   BOATING AND SWIMMING   226
   SAFE WATER BY THE WAY   229

   GLOSSARY   232
   INDEX   241

Unit I

HOW TO HAVE FEWER COLDS

"Why is Bill absent?"

A cold very likely. Most of the absences from school and from work are caused by colds.

Colds are something to fight. We must work hard to prevent them. Say now, "I'm going to have fewer colds this year."

Read this unit to find out why and how to fight colds.

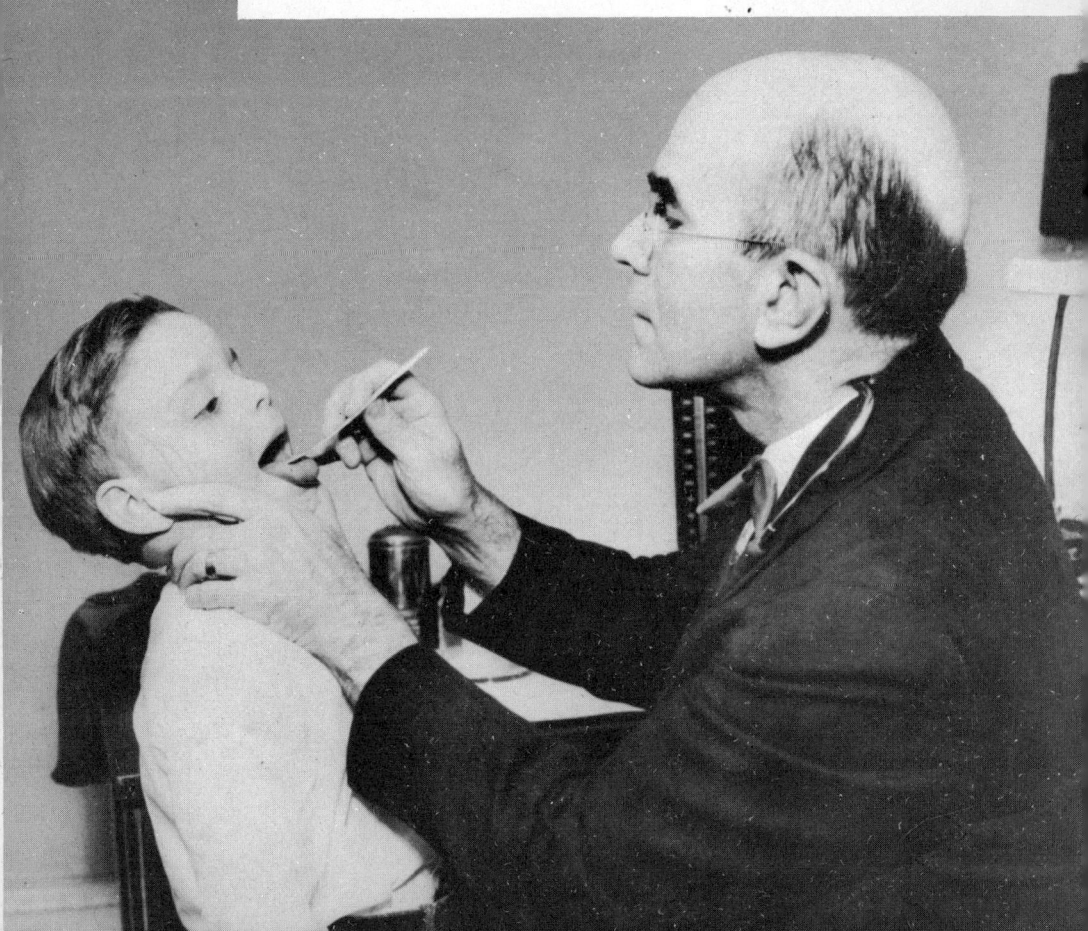

OUTDOOR FUN HELPS PREVENT COLDS.

COLDS SPOIL THE FUN

If you have a cold, other people are afraid of catching it. You yourself may feel sick all over. A cold may spoil all the fun you have been planning to have. It may keep you at home by yourself when the other children are out playing.

Ted had planned to go mountain climbing, but a cold spoiled his fun. His head ached, his throat was sore, and his nose was running. His mother sent for the doctor. She knew Ted had a fever * and that there was a case of scarlet * fever among his friends at school.

"Ted has a bad cold," the doctor said. "But I don't think it is going to be anything more serious. Keep him in bed several days. Give him plenty of water and orange juice and simple foods like milk toast, cream of spinach soup, baked potato, custard,* and junket.* Telephone me how he is coming along."

So Ted stayed in bed for several days. This gave his body a better chance to fight the cold. And he kept his cold to himself.

When the doctor said Ted could go out, he went back to school. Bill told him about the fun he had missed.

"No more colds for me if I can help it!" Ted said.

"No more colds for me if I can help it!" said

* You can look up the meaning of all starred (*) words in the glossary at the end of the book.

Jane. "I missed all the fun because of a sore throat."

"Let's try to find out how to prevent colds," said Ted. "I'd like to know what causes colds, how colds are spread, how to try to prevent colds, and how to cure colds."

GERMS * THAT CAUSE COLDS

Colds are caused by germs. *"Bacteria"* * is the scientist's * name for some kinds of germs.

Have you ever seen bacteria under a microscope? * They are most like very small plants. When these small living things have food, water, and warmth, they split in two. Each half becomes a new bacterium. Soon there are thousands of bacteria where there was only one to begin with.

Some colds are caused by germs even smaller than bacteria. You could not see them even with an ordinary microscope. The right name for these very small germs is *viruses*.* Bacteria, the larger germs, and viruses, the smaller germs, behave in about the same way.

HOW COLDS ARE SPREAD

Have you noticed how often, when your father comes home with a cold, you and your mother soon catch it, too? Have you noticed how often, when someone comes to school with a cold, half

1

HOW BACTERIA AND VIRUSES GET INTO THE AIR

The cloud of droplets in picture 1 is sent out by a big sneeze. The large droplets may go as far as 12 feet; the smaller ones may go much farther.

In picture 2, on page 6, the mouth is not open so wide. What changes do you see in the droplets? The bacteria and viruses, you know, ride into the air on the droplets.

Look at pictures 3 and 4 on page 6. What effect does covering the mouth have on the number of droplets sent into the air?

Why is catching a sneeze in a handkerchief better than catching it in the hand?

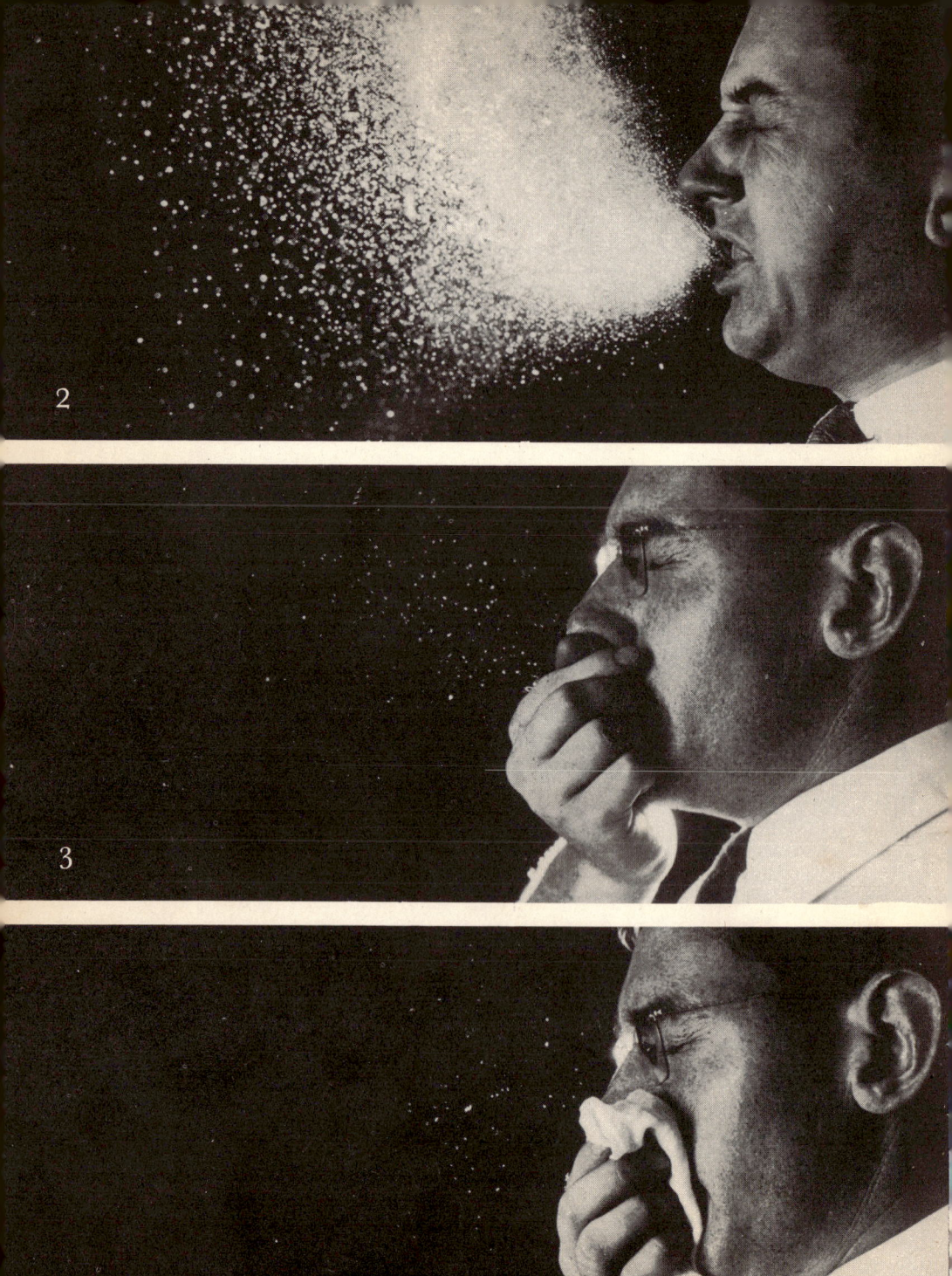

the class are soon coughing and sneezing and blowing their noses?

The careless person with a cold can spread his germs in many ways. When a person does not cover his sneezes or coughs, the spray is sent to other people's faces. If he is at the table, it gets on the food, too. The bacteria and viruses in the spray may get on hands, towels, pencils, and anything else he touches. Spray spreads.

WAYS TO PREVENT AND CURE COLDS

Knowing how germs are spread helps us to keep from having colds. Here are ways we can try to keep colds away from others and from ourselves:

1. Keep six feet away from a person who coughs and sneezes without covering his nose and mouth. Colds are most catching the first few days. Do not go to the movies or other crowded places when colds are "in the air."

2. Do not eat fruit or any other kind of food that may be offered to you by others after they have taken bites out of it.

3. Do not eat food that has been standing without a cover on it. Wash raw fruit well before eating it.

4. Help people you know to form the habit of always sneezing and coughing into a handkerchief. And be sure you have the habit yourself!

5. Do not borrow other children's pencils,

handkerchiefs, whistles, towels, or other things that you might put in your mouth or up to your face.

6. Always wash your hands and face before eating and after being in crowds.

7. If you have a bad cold, use soft paper handkerchiefs or napkins or small pieces of old, clean cloth instead of other handkerchiefs. You can burn the paper handkerchiefs and old cloths as soon as you have used them.

8. Rest in bed, eat lightly, and drink plenty of water and fruit juice the first two or three days of a cold and fever.

9. Have your throat and nose examined to see whether bacteria are making their home in your tonsils * or whether you have adenoids * in the back part of your nose. Diseased tonsils and adenoid growths may make trouble at any time. Some boys and girls have fewer colds after these nests of bacteria are removed.

Read over the rules again carefully and show how each of them helps to keep germs out of your nose and throat. Help other children to keep these rules.

It is impossible for a person to keep all kinds of germs out of his nose and throat. In fact, a wise person would not try to do this, because he would then be thinking about germs all the time.

But we try to do everything that will make it hard for the harmful viruses and bacteria to make us ill.

Doctors believe that we can do some things to give our bodies the best chance to resist * colds. Here are the most important things to do:

1. Play or work out of doors every day. Being out in the sunshine and active in the cold air helps to prevent colds. But do not get chilled by wearing too little clothing, by sitting in a draft,* by wearing wet shoes or clothing, or by cooling off too quickly when you are perspiring * after exercise. Wearing too much clothing is as bad as wearing too little. Wear just enough to keep comfortably warm.

2. Take a cool splash in the morning if it agrees with you. Cool baths help some people to prevent colds. A cool bath in the morning helps the skin to become used to sudden changes in temperature.* Then a person can go from a warm room to a cold place without feeling chilly. A cool-air bath does the same thing and is better for some people than a cool-water bath. If you feel good and warm after a cool bath, it shows that the cool bath agrees with you. If you feel cold and uncomfortable, it shows that the cool bath does not agree with you.

3. Keep heated rooms at just the right temperature. The temperature of the rooms in which you live is important in preventing colds. Scientists found that school children in rooms in which the temperature was kept at about 68° (68 degrees) had fewer colds than children in rooms that were heated to over 70°.

4. Try to live and work where the air is fresh and clean. Dust and smoke may irritate * the nose and throat and so make catching cold easier.

5. Drink plenty of water and eat the "protective * foods." Drinking four or more glasses of water a day seems to help prevent as well as cure colds. Many people seem to have fewer colds when they eat more fruit and vegetables and less bread and sweets. A teaspoonful of cod-liver * or other fish oil or A and D vitamins * in something else, if taken every day in the dark months, help to increase one's resistance * to colds.

6. Regular bowel * movements seem to help prevent colds. One of the questions a doctor asks a person with a bad cold is, "Have your bowels moved regularly?" If you eat vegetables, fruits, and whole cereals and if you set aside a regular time each day for a bowel movement, the bowels will usually take care of themselves.

7. Get enough rest and sleep. Fatigue * is your enemy. It is on the side of viruses and bacteria. So, to help prevent colds, get plenty of rest and sleep. An eight o'clock bedtime means that your body will be sure to get enough rest. If you take care of your body, it will take care of the viruses and bacteria if there are not too many of them.

As you have read these pages, did you think to yourself, "So many things to do to prevent colds"? But did you notice something? The things that help prevent colds are the same things that help to keep you well in other ways.

Make a plan for the day to help you keep from catching cold. See how really easy such a plan is to follow and how good it makes you feel. And besides—it will help to keep you from missing football and baseball games, trips, picnics, parties, and the circus.

If you follow your plan and you do catch a cold, probably it will not be a bad one. Remember how to take care of yourself. Stay at home, rest in bed, drink glasses and glasses of water and fruit juice, and eat simple foods. By simple foods we mean milk toast, cream vegetable soups, baked potato, custard, and junket. Simple foods like these are best to eat every day.

Other Children's Questions

What are the right answers to these questions, which other children have asked?
1. How could a person give us his cold?
2. How can we keep our cold from spreading?
3. Why should we stay at home if we have a bad cold?

Which Answer Is Best?

1. When you sneeze or cough,
    cover your nose and mouth with your hand.
    cover your nose and mouth with a paper handkerchief.
    turn your head and do not bother to cover your nose and mouth.
2. When you wash your face and hands,
    use your brother's towel.
    use a friend's towel.
    use your own towel.
3. When you have a cold,
    take cough drops often.
    eat a big dinner of meat, potatoes, bread and butter, and pie.
    drink glasses and glasses of water and fruit juice.
4. Bacteria are most like
    tiny animals.
    very small plants.
    harmful bugs.
5. Bacteria grow very fast in
    cold, dry places.
    dusty, outdoor air.
    warm, moist food.

Things to Do

1. Do you want to join the "Cold Fighters"? Then make a daily plan for yourself. Put into the plan all the rules for preventing colds that you have read in this unit. Follow your plan every day.

2. Some of the things you do to prevent colds also help to prevent measles,* mumps,* scarlet fever, chicken * pox, and other diseases which school children sometimes catch. What do you think these things are?

3. Tell your father and mother about viruses and bacteria and ways of preventing colds.

4. If there is a baby in your family, try to protect him from colds.

5. Watch the thermometer * in your classroom. How can you keep the temperature at about 68°?

6. Be out of doors in the sunlight as much as is healthful in your part of the country. Put on your sweater when you rest after exercising. Remind other children to put on their sweaters.

7. Make titles for the pictures on page 11.

8. Find the health words in this unit. Each one has a star (*) after it the first time it is used in this book. Definitions of the starred words are given in the glossary, which begins on page 232. Find the first starred word, *fever,* in the glossary, page 236. Make a dictionary by cutting the edges of a notebook so that you have a place for each letter of the alphabet. Find the first *F* page in your dictionary and write at the top, *fever.* Write the meaning of this word and a sentence or two using it. On the page paste pictures and clippings you find about preventing or getting over a fever. In the same way put the other starred words in this unit in your dictionary. If you do this for each unit, you will soon have a book of your own. It will be your Health Dictionary. Later, if you do not clearly remember any of these words, you can look them up in your dictionary.

Unit II

NEW WAYS FOR OLD

Look at the children in the picture on this page. Should you like to have them for your friends?

Some children are happy and friendly all the time. Some children are often unhappy or cross. And some children have learned to make and to do things that bring happiness.

Did you ever get over being afraid of something? How did you do it? In this unit you will find out how some boys and girls changed old ways of acting to new and better ways. Have you discovered ways of growing happier, friendlier, or braver?

HAPPY WITH A HOBBY

HOW SALLY CHANGED

One day a farmer stopped his truck in front of Sally's house. In the truck was a small gray burro. Sally jumped up and down for joy.

"Here she is," said the farmer. "Her name is Silky. She looks ragged now in her winter coat, but it will shine like silk before July."

Silky was led down a wide board and into Sally's yard. Sally's mother and father, her big sister, and her little brother came out to see Silky.

Sally was very happy. She patted and patted the burro, first on the long nose, then on the rough sides.

Silky seemed to feel at home. She was used to many places, many people. She ate the early spring grass calmly. She seemed to like green grass better than anything else.

Inside the house Sally's mother said to her father, "I've never seen Sally so happy. Now I know she will stay out of doors. This summer will not be like last summer, when she wanted to play indoors all the time. She lost weight last summer and has gained only a little since."

"I bet that Sally will get a good coat of tan this year," said Sally's father. "She will be glad to eat everything on her plate at every meal. She will sleep like a top. She will stand tall, in good posture.* I know, because that's what selling papers did for me when I was Sally's age."

17

"And that's what ten chickens did for me when I was ten," said Sally's mother.

"But, if Sally has the burro, she will have no time to make friends," said Sally's big sister. "I think she should play more with other children."

"I think the burro will bring Sally friends, too," said her father. "Selling papers kept me busy out of doors, and it brought me new friends."

The next day Sally rode Silky over to the corral at the edge of town. This was a big, fenced-in field with an old barn at one end. Here Silky was to live.

Sally rode Silky round and round the corral. Soon they knew every part of Silky's new home.

A boy and a girl looked over the fence.

"Hello," said one. "What's your burro's name?"

"Silky," Sally told them. "What are your names?"

"Tommy," said the boy.

"Jenny," said the girl.

"My name is Sally Rush. Do you want to ride Silky around the corral?" she asked.

"Yes," they said as they climbed over the fence.

After they had each had a ride, Sally said, "Let's give Silky a rest."

Then Sally brought Silky hay and oats and a pail of water. Silky ate the oats and hay quietly. Food was all she seemed to care about.

After eating and then drinking the water, the burro rolled over and over in the dry dust.

FRIENDS THE BURRO BROUGHT

"That's a burro's way of taking a bath," said Tommy, laughing.

Sally ran for a stiff brush that she had bought. She gave Silky a good brushing all over.

"Look at all the hair that came out!" she exclaimed.

"She's losing her winter coat," said Tommy. "She couldn't stand all that hair in summer; so she sheds it. Next fall she will get a new coat for winter."

"Only people have to worry about winter clothes, and summer clothes, and clothes for wet weather," said Jenny.

After school and on week ends Sally, Tommy, and Jenny had fun with the burro. On some week ends the two friends helped Sally take the burro from the corral to her yard. There the burro ate green grass all day. Sally was careful to keep the yard clean. She did not want to bring flies around.

Other children came to ride the burro. Little Brother of course had many rides. Sally was very careful of the smaller children.

"Silky might kick," she told them. "So never go near her heels. Never do anything to frighten or hurt her."

One Saturday morning Sally's big sister said, "There are seven children in the yard. Silky has brought Sally many friends."

"I am glad the children come," said Sally's mother. "Sally is happy to have them come. Have you seen how tanned she is getting, how red her cheeks are, how her eyes shine? She eats and sleeps well now. She wants a big glass of milk at every meal. She even is willing to take an hour's rest before dinner and go to bed at eight o'clock. She is gaining weight. And her muscles * are firm."

One evening Sally's father said, "I like the tall way you walk and sit. I am proud of the way you sit tall at the table."

"I *feel* taller," said Sally.

One June day Sally sat on the top of the corral fence with Tommy and Jenny.

"I brought a big lunch today, of egg sandwiches and fruit—enough for all of us," said Sally. "I will go and get it."

Sally went to get her lunch. She came back without it.

"What do you think?" she said. "Silky ate our lunch, paper bag and everything. Let's go to my house for lunch."

The three of them got on their bicycles. They did not forget any of the rules for riding bicycles safely. They kept to the right side of the street. They slowed down at crossings. They held out their hand when they made a turn.

"Riding a burro is different from riding a bicycle," said Sally. "A green light means 'Go' to a person, while green grass means 'Stop' for a burro."

When they reached Sally's house, they went to

the kitchen. Mother laughed and helped them get lunch. They had brown bread and butter; a salad of apples, celery, and raisins; and milk to drink.

One July morning when Sally came back from the corral, she cried, "Mother, Father, Silky has a colt. It's so little. It lies on the straw, and Silky stays right by it. Silky let me touch her colt, but she would not let anyone else come near it."

Later in the day Sally and her family got in the car and went to see the colt.

"It looks like a little deer," said Sally's mother.

"It's lovely," said Sally's big sister.

"It's mine," said Little Brother.

"When it gets big and strong and you are a little bigger and stronger, you can ride it," said Sally. "Then it will be yours. Right now the colt belongs to Silky."

The little colt got up on its long legs and wobbled toward Sally.

"I will name you Rocket," said Sally, "because you are going to be a fast-running burro. You can walk the day you are born."

Rocket was a good name for the colt. Before he was a week old, he was running round and round the corral. He would kick with his back feet as he ran. He was a funny sight. After he had run a little while he would lie down and rest. Sally rested in the sunshine with him. During the heat at noon he rested on the straw in the barn.

Rocket drank only Silky's milk the first two

weeks. Then he began to take a little water from the pail. When he was three weeks old, he began to eat grass. Soon he was eating oats also.

How he grew! By September he was twice as big as he had been in July.

When Sally went back to school in September, there was much that she wanted to tell her teacher. But the teacher spoke first.

"Sally," she exclaimed, "what has happened to you? You have grown in height and weight. You are so brown, so strong, so straight and tall. You are the picture of health!"

"Silky and Rocket have made me over," Sally told her. "I'm an outdoor girl now. Oh, you must come down to the corral some day to see Silky and Rocket, my burros."

Questions to Answer

1. In which of these ways did Sally change?
    - (1) She gained in weight.
    - (2) She sat and stood taller.
    - (3) She cried oftener.
    - (4) She had more color in her cheeks.
    - (5) Her eyes were brighter.
    - (6) She became tanned by the sun.
    - (7) She spent all her time with the burro and never played with other children.
    - (8) She walked with her head forward.
    - (9) She went to bed at nine o'clock.
    - (10) She made new friends.

2. Do you know what made Sally different? Write what you think on a piece of paper. Then see if you thought of the same things that are listed here:

    Sally spent her afternoons and week ends out of doors.
    She enjoyed two good kinds of exercise.
    Outdoor exercise gave her an appetite for her meals.
    She drank at least three glasses of milk each day.
    She took an hour's rest before dinner.
    She went to bed at eight o'clock.
    She had a pet of her own to love and care for.
    She was happy with her friends.
    She was happy with her family.

WHO'S AFRAID?

Everyone is afraid of something. Even brave people are afraid sometimes. It is better to be careful and a little bit afraid than to do foolish, dangerous things. We should not laugh at other people who are afraid, even though we think their fears are silly. We should try to find out what makes us afraid. Then we may find some way to get over our fears.

Here are three stories about boys and girls who were afraid and what they did about it.

HOW DONALD LEARNED TO LIKE THE WATER

Donald had been afraid of the water ever since he was a baby. He did not know why he was afraid. Still he did not like to go into a lake or an ocean. He did not even like to take a trip on a big boat though his mother told him that it was almost as safe as a house.

Donald's mother and father did not try to make him go in swimming or take boat trips. Instead, they went to a farm or to the mountains for their vacations. There Donald could ride horseback and climb trees and play games. All summer long he never even thought of swimming or taking boat trips.

But one year he went away to camp. Then the

25

trouble began. The camp was on a lake, and swimming was one of the most popular sports.

Donald did not want to tell anyone he was afraid of the water. He thought he would just take a sun bath and maybe go wading. So when it came time for swimming the first day, he put on his bathing suit and went down to the lake with the boys and Gordon, the swimming teacher. Gordon was a college boy and a fine swimmer himself. But best of all he was kind and understanding. He seemed to know just how other people felt and how they liked to be treated.

Donald walked into the water a little way, and suddenly his old fear of the water came over him. He could not shake it off. He stood there in the shallow water, while the other boys swam and splashed and dived in water over their heads.

Three older boys saw Donald standing there and called, "Come on in; the water's fine." Donald just stood there and shook his head, and the boys knew that he was afraid.

"Let's duck him," Bill said; and before Donald knew what was happening, three of the boys had picked him up and were carrying him into the deep water.

Just then Gordon came over. "What's this, a ducking party?" he asked. "I didn't see a ducking party on the program of events for this morning. Did you?

"And, Bill, do you remember last summer when you were afraid of horses and did not want to learn to ride? Did we put you on the wildest horse and send him galloping down the road? As I remember it, we put you on Star, who is as gentle as a kitten, and walked around and around the ring with you on Star's back. After a few days you did not need me when Star walked with you on her back. Then I rode beside you, and we let the horses trot around the ring."

Bill grinned. "I see your point all right, Gordon. Ducking a fellow isn't the best way to teach him to swim."

"It's the worst way," said Gordon. "So we don't do it at this camp."

The other boys went back to their swimming and diving, leaving Donald alone with Gordon.

"When you learn to swim, Donald," Gordon told him, "you will not be afraid of the water. We are not afraid of things we have learned to control."

Then Gordon showed Donald how to breathe with his face in the water part of the time. By the end of the hour Donald had learned how to breathe in when his head was turned to the side and to breathe out when his face was under water.

On the next days Gordon showed Donald how to do the dead man's float, face down in the water; how to float on his back; and how to keep afloat by treading water, that is, stepping quickly up and down in deep water. As long as Gordon was beside him, Donald was not afraid. Soon he had learned to keep afloat as long as he wanted to and was ready to learn to swim.

During the summer Donald learned to swim fifty yards in good form and won the swimming medal for beginners. With his gain in control over the water, he lost his fear of it. His mother and father thought that getting over his fear of the water was the best thing he had learned at camp. They bought him a ticket for an indoor swimming pool so that he could go swimming all winter. Now when Donald's family goes on a vacation, they always choose a place where Donald will have a chance to swim.

WHAT PATTY LEARNED FROM HER LITTLE BROTHER

As far back as she could remember, Patty had been afraid of the dark. Time and again her mother went into her room with her, turned on the light, and showed her that there was nothing to fear.

"See, Patty," she would say, laughing, "there are no bears in the closet or boogymen under the bed."

And Patty would say, "I know it's silly to be afraid, but I just can't help it."

One dark, winter afternoon Patty heard her three-year-old brother, Teddy, crying. She went to see what was the matter. She found that his ball had rolled into a dark room and that he was afraid to go into the room and get it.

Patty laughed and said, "Let's go and find the ball together." Patty knew just where the light was, and she showed Teddy the cord hanging down from it. "Pull this cord, Teddy," she said, "and the light will come on."

Teddy pulled the cord. Then the room became as bright as day.

Teddy laughed. "Again," he said. So he pulled the cord again and brought on darkness. Then he pulled the cord again and made the room light. He did this three or four times before he thought of his ball.

They found the ball and played with it for a few minutes. Then Patty let Teddy turn off the light, and they walked out of the dark room.

Once more the ball rolled into the dark.

"You get it," Patty said to Teddy.

"Patty come, too," said Teddy.

"Patty will come, but Teddy will find the light and turn it on," she said.

Patty showed Teddy how to feel his way to the

light. She pointed out the shining end of the cord. Teddy pulled it. The room became bright, and he found his ball.

In this way Patty taught Teddy how to find his way in a dark room without being afraid. "And," she told her mother that evening, "I've taught myself also not to be afraid of the dark."

JEAN, AFRAID OF DOGS

When Jean was two years old, she was playing out of doors when a big dog came along. He was really only a puppy, and he ran up to her barking and frisking in a puppy's friendly way. He wanted to play. Jean had just learned to walk and was still unsteady on her feet. As the big, clumsy puppy pranced against her, he knocked her over. Jean was badly frightened and began to cry.

Since that time Jean had been afraid of dogs of all kinds, big or little. Her mother and father told her that the dogs she met would not hurt her if she did not tease them. Still Jean was afraid of dogs and stayed as far away from them as possible.

Other children began to notice that Jean was afraid of dogs, and they teased her about it. Their teasing did not help Jean to get over her fear of dogs. It only made her unhappy. She began to play by herself and missed many good times.

Then one day her father bought a tiny white puppy. He was so little and helpless that Jean fell in love with him at once. She named him Whitie because he was so very white.

She learned how to take care of him and what food to give him. Very young puppies should have five meals every day. Two meals should be of milk mixed with toast or dry cereal; and three should be of chopped raw, lean beef, mixed with dry bread or cereal. Jean fed Whitie at the right times every day. Besides his food, she also gave him some fish-liver oil every day. She kept his water dish clean and full of fresh water. She took him out of doors at least four times a day at the same time each day. If anyone wanted to feed Whitie small bones, she said that puppies should never be given fishbones or other small bones.

Whitie let Jean do anything she wanted with him. He even let her dress him up in doll's clothes—a red cape and black hat. In those clothes he looked so funny that Jean couldn't help laughing. Whitie barked and barked and was glad when Jean took off the doll's clothes.

When Jean went on the street, she always put a muzzle on Whitie even though he did not like it. He would scratch and scratch with his little paw, trying to get the muzzle off. "No, no, Whitie," Jean would say. "It's the law for dogs to wear muzzles on the street, and we must obey the law."

Jean did not pet strange dogs, and she stayed away from dogs without muzzles. But the more she played with Whitie and learned how to take care of him,

33

the better she liked dogs. After a while she was not afraid of any friendly dogs she met.

Questions to Answer

1. What is the difference between being afraid and being careful? Read the sentences below. Which of the children were being careful? Which were being afraid?

(1) David stayed in shallow water until he had learned to swim.

(2) Dick went swimming in a pond where he had never been before. Instead of diving right in he walked out as far as he could go and swam back.

(3) Betty would not go to sleep without having a light on in her room.

(4) Helen carefully felt her way into a dark room until she found the cord for the light.

(5) Jane did not pet strange dogs or go near strange dogs without muzzles.

(6) Anne would scream or cry if a dog came near her.

(7) Peter looked both ways before crossing the street.

(8) George would not cross a street by himself.

2. What is one of the best ways to get over being afraid of something that really will not hurt you?

3. What is the best way to meet dangers, like lightning, which we cannot control?

4. Why do we no longer have to be afraid of darkness, as people used to be?

Things to Do

1. Help a little child whom you know to get over his fear of something that will not harm him.

2. If you are afraid of something that really will not hurt you, try to get over your fear, as Donald, Patty, and Jean got over their fears.

WHEN YOU MAKE A MISTAKE

How often do you hear people say, "Excuse me," or, "I'm sorry"? That is what we should say when we make mistakes. It is still better not to make mistakes. Of course we all make mistakes sometimes, but we can learn not to make the same mistake twice. How silly it would be if we had to go about saying, "Excuse me," all the time just because we kept making the same old mistake!

These stories are about Jack and Bill. They tell about mistakes the two boys made and how they learned not to make the same ones twice.

JACK FACES HIS LOW MARK IN ARITHMETIC

Jack made many mistakes on his arithmetic test, and his mark was very low. At first he felt angry at the teacher for giving him such a low mark. "She is always picking on me," he thought. Then he began to wonder whether or not the low mark might have been his own fault. He decided to ask his teacher about it.

"Why did I get such a low mark in arithmetic?" he asked.

"That's the right question to ask, Jack," Miss Brown said. "Bring me your arithmetic paper and we will try to find out why you made the mistakes on it."

Jack got his arithmetic paper, and together they tried to see why he had made each mistake. The first mistake was caused by his not knowing that 9 times 7 is 63. Jack added 9 sevens and saw that they made 63. He felt sure that he would never miss 9 times 7 again.

Three mistakes were in reading the problems. "When you read a problem," Miss Brown told him, "try to find out what is given in the problem, what is to be found, and what you must do to find it—whether you have to add, multiply, divide, or subtract.

"Here are some problems like the ones in the test. Read them to find out what to do. You need not do the figuring; just find out what figuring you should do to get the answers."

Jack did as Miss Brown said.

Every day Miss Brown gave Jack problems to read in this way until he learned to see just what was given and what was to be found and what figuring was necessary. After he had learned to read problems correctly, he had no trouble in getting the right answers.

On the next test Jack made some mistakes, but not so many and not the same kinds as before. He learned from these mistakes, too. That was why his marks in arithmetic slowly climbed higher and higher as the year went on.

BILL FINDS A BETTER WAY

One day when Bill came home after school, he found that his older Brother, Fred, had taken his bicycle. So Bill took Fred's baseball and bat and was soon having a lively game of baseball with some of his friends.

When Fred came home a little later, he wanted his baseball and bat. He couldn't find them anywhere.

"Maybe Bill took them," his mother said.

Fred went over to the baseball field and, sure enough, there were Bill and his friends playing with Fred's ball and bat.

Fred went up to Bill. "Say, Bill, I want my ball and bat. Hand them over, will you?"

"No," said Bill. "You had my bicycle; so I took your ball and bat. We have just begun a game."

"Well, my team is waiting for me, and I must have my ball and bat."

"I had to wait for my bicycle. You can just wait for your ball and bat," said Bill.

"I will not," said Fred. They were both getting angry.

Then Bill had an idea. "Bring your team over here, Fred, and we will play with them."

Fred thought to himself: "Some of those fellows are pretty good players. Maybe it would be fun to play Bill's team."

"All right," he said. "We will be over in a few minutes."

"Hurray," shouted Bill's friends. They were delighted to have the chance to play with the older team.

Both teams had fun. Of course Fred's team won, but Bill's team made them work for every score. Everyone had a good afternoon.

Questions to Answer

1. Can you think of some mistakes the boys did *not* make? If you can, write them in your health notebook.
2. Which do you think are more important—the mistakes Jack and Bill did make or the ones they did not make? Why do you think so?
3. How did Jack learn not to make his mistakes in arithmetic again?
4. Can you think of a mistake that you used to make that you don't make any more?
5. Can you remember a time when
    (1) someone blamed you for something you did not do?
    (2) you got a low mark in school?
    (3) your brother or sister took something that belonged to you?

What did you do? Do you think you could have done something better?

Things to Do

1. If you find a quarrel beginning, try to find a way out that will please everyone. Instead of fighting or sulking, it is much better to settle a quarrel so that everyone may then have a good time.
2. The next time you make a mistake, use it as a chance to learn not to make that mistake again.

If you get a low mark on your test or on your report card, do not blame someone else for the low mark. Instead, try to think of all the reasons why your mark was low. If you cannot find the reasons, ask someone to help you find out the best thing for you to do.

WHO'S POPULAR?

Being popular means being liked by many people or having many friends. Almost everyone wants to be popular. How does it happen that some boys and girls are popular and others are not? Is there something magic about being popular? Or can anyone become popular? The popular boy or girl is the one who—but read these stories and find out for yourself. After you have read them, you may be able to think of other reasons why a boy or girl is popular or unpopular—liked or disliked by others.

THANKS TO MARY

The boys and girls in Mary's class were having a surprise party for Betty. The presents they had brought for her were tucked into a big red umbrella. The orange juice was in a pitcher in the icebox, and the cake with pink icing was safe in a clean tin cake box. Betty would be there any minute. As soon as they heard the doorbell ring, they were going to run and hide in their places. Betty would have a big surprise.

Just then someone said: "Oh, dear! We forgot to get the paper cups for the orange juice. Now what shall we do?"

For a minute no one spoke. They just looked at one another.

Then Mary said, "I'll run to the store and get the paper cups."

Now the store was five blocks away, and everyone knew that part of the fun would be over by the time Mary got back. The boys and girls told her so.

"Oh," said Mary, "someone has to go. We can't drink out of the pitcher. I'll hurry." So she put on her coat and hat and went to the store.

The party had already begun when she got back. She slipped into the game they were playing, and the party went on merrily.

Later they each had a piece of cake and a clean paper cup full of delicious orange juice. "Thanks to Mary," someone said.

CHOSEN BY THE CLASS

The class was planning a play day. They had invited boys and girls from four schools to come and play games with them.

The first step in planning was to choose committees. One committee would plan the games.

43

Another committee would write the invitations and make all the boys and girls feel welcome. Another committee would plan the lunch hour.

They decided to choose the head of each committee by a vote. Then he could choose other boys and girls to work with him.

"I think Tom would be a good person to plan the games," said Bob. "He knows how to play many games. He knows how to get things done, and he always gets them done on time."

Dick looked around the room. He had been hoping someone would choose him. He liked to be on committees. Then he remembered what had happened the month before. He had been helping on the library committee. His job was to keep track of all the books brought back to the library. For the first week he had done good work. Then he forgot to be on hand to take in the books. He even put three of the best books in his own desk instead of putting them back on the shelf. After that, no one would want to choose him!

Everyone in the class voted for Tom. Then they waited to see whom he would choose to work with him.

"I choose Patty and Jane and Dick," said Tom. "We shall need ideas from the class and their help in getting things done. I think we should begin planning right away."

Dick could hardly believe that Tom had really chosen him. But that was another good thing about

Tom. He was always willing to let a fellow have a second chance.

The class chose the heads of the other committees. Soon they were all at work trying to make their play day a big success.

What Do You Think?

Read these things that boys and girls sometimes do. Write on a piece of paper all of them that you think make boys and girls well liked by others.

1. Take things that do not belong to them
2. Tell lies
3. Do their part
4. Cheat
5. Keep a secret
6. Tell the truth
7. Stay with a friend in trouble
8. Try to get out of things
9. Bully smaller children
10. Show they can be trusted
11. Help others
12. Stop playing when they are about to lose
13. Mind their own business
14. Show they are good losers
15. Call people names
16. Make fun of people
17. Make fun of poor people's clothing
18. Control their tempers
19. Tell tales on others
20. Own up when they are wrong

Questions to Answer

1. What did Mary gain by going to the store for paper cups? What did she lose? Which do you think is more important?

2. Do you think Tom deserved to be chosen for the committee? Why? Did Dick? Why?

3. What do you think makes a boy or girl popular? What makes a boy or girl unpopular?

Things to Do

1. Try to treat other boys and girls as you would like to be treated yourself. Try to put yourself in their place.

2. If you are chosen as head of a committee, begin work the way Tom did.

3. Form a Big Brother or Big Sister Club. The members of this club help to take good care of young children. Learn games, stories, and songs that young children will like. Help them to be careful but not afraid. If they get into trouble, help them to find the best way out. Don't do everything for them; help them to learn to do things for themselves.

Which Is Better?

1. If a child is afraid of the water—
    (1) To duck him in fun?
    (2) To teach him to float and swim?
2. If a child is afraid of the dark—
    (1) To tell him it is silly to be afraid of the dark?
    (2) To take a flashlight and show him that there is nothing to hurt him in the dark place?
3. If a child is afraid of germs—
    (1) To tell him about the harm some germs do?
    (2) To teach him how to protect himself and others from germs?
4. If a child is not popular with other children—
    (1) To tell him he ought to have more friends?
    (2) To find ways in which he can help the group?

Unit III

HEALTHFUL DAYS

Think of the happiest days you have had. What made them happy?

Think of the most unhappy days you have had. What made them unhappy? How could they have been made happier?

Is it hard for you to find time to do the things you want most to do? Do you find that you are too tired to do the things you want to do? Do you have trouble being strong enough to do the things you want to do?

Read this unit to find out how other children solved some of their problems. Perhaps it will help you with one of your problems.

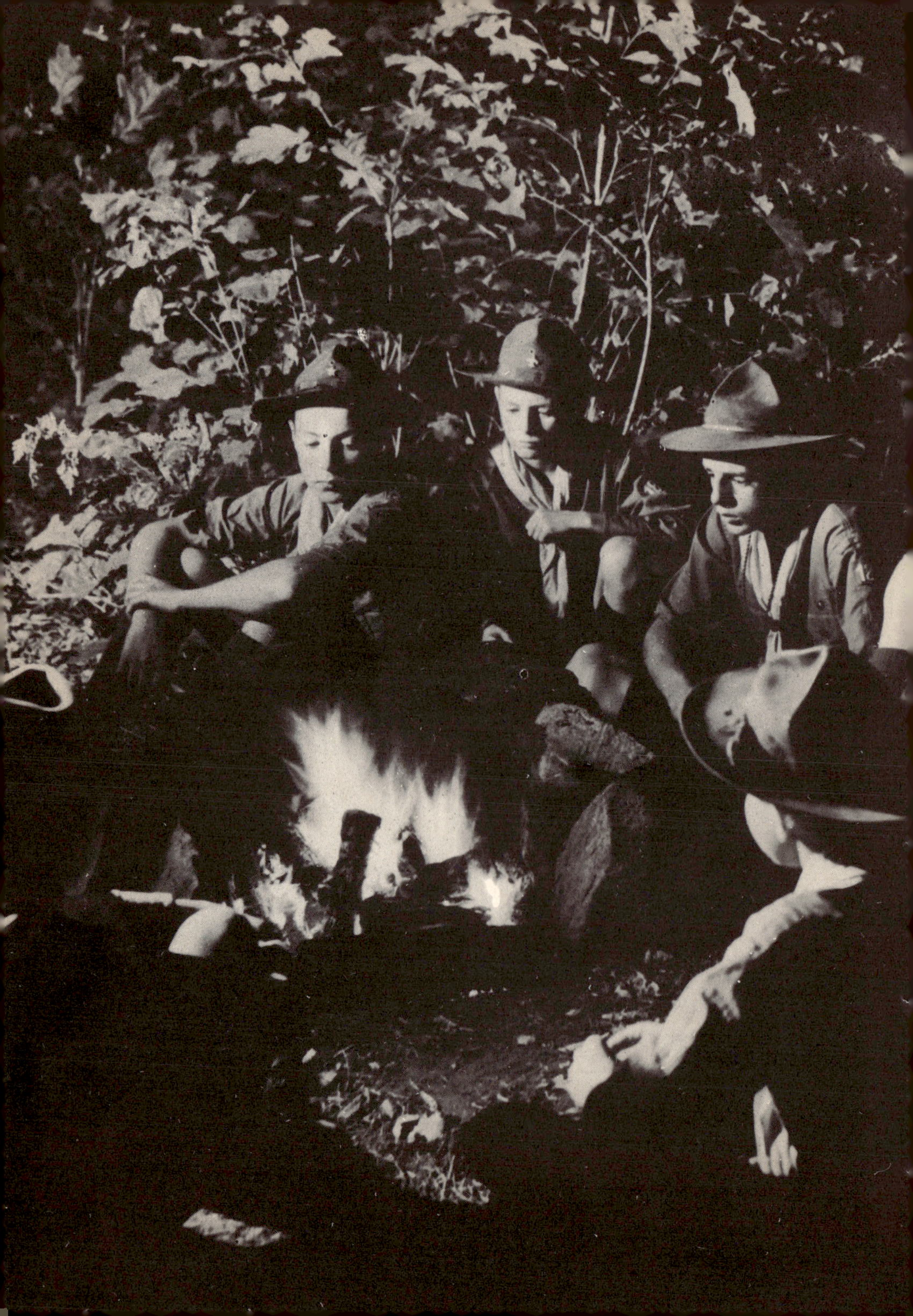

HOW TO FIND TIME TO DO THE THINGS YOU WANT TO DO

HOW BILL FOUND TIME AT HOME

One autumn day Bill said, "At camp last summer we had time for everything we wanted to do. But at home I never have time to do all the things I want to do."

"Why not bring camp life home?" his father asked. "Tell me about your camp days. Perhaps you can have some camp fun while you are at home."

"At camp," Bill began, "we had regular hours for doing things. We got up at seven o'clock and were ready for breakfast by half past seven.

"After breakfast we made our beds and put our tents in order. Then we had the morning hours for nature study and handcraft. The swimming hour came before dinner.

"After dinner we had a quiet hour. Games or hikes came later in the afternoon. Supper was at six o'clock.

"As soon as supper was over, we played games around the campfire. Sometimes the head of the camp, whom we called Big Chief, told us stories about Indians and wild animals. It was almost dark when we left the campfire to go back to our tents."

"Did you have a regular bedtime, too?" asked Bill's father. "A day like that made you ready for bed, didn't it?"

"It did," said Bill. "When the bugle sounded taps at eight o'clock, everyone had settled down for a good night's sleep. There was no noise after taps because all the boys knew it was time to be quiet then. Besides, we were all sleepy and wanted to rest up for the next day. Big Chief said that he did not want tired campers around. They are usually cross and do not enjoy camp fun."

"It seems to me," said Father, "that your time in camp was well planned. Don't you think that you could make your days now very much like camp days?"

"Of course I could!" cried Bill. "The only changes I would have to make would be to put schoolwork in place of nature study and handcraft and part of the afternoon games. But after school I can play many of the games we played in camp. I can skate and take hikes in winter."

"And save a little time to go to the store for Mother, or cut the grass, or rake up leaves, or do other chores?" his father asked.

Bill said he would save a certain time every day to help at home. He thought the best time would be the hour before supper, after he had been playing. Father agreed that would be a good time.

"Instead of sitting around the campfire after supper," Bill continued, "I can listen to the radio or do my homework. I'll try it, Dad. It seems as though I ought to have time for everything."

"I think you will," said his father. "A planned

day always seems to have more time in it. See if you can make a plan for your days at home."

BILL'S SCHEDULE *

Bill wrote a schedule for days at home that was very much like the summer camp schedule. Here is his schedule:

MORNING

7:00	Get up, wash, and dress
7:30	Eat breakfast
8:00	Make bed and put room in order
8:30	Walk to school
9:00	Work in school

NOON

   12:00   Lunch hour

AFTERNOON
AND EVENING

   1:00   Work in school
   3:00   Play games out of doors or go on hikes
   5:00   Do chores for Father and Mother
   6:00   Eat supper
   7:00   Time for myself to talk or read or study or just relax *
   7:45   Get ready for bed
   8:15   Asleep

Do you think Bill had a good plan for his school days? Can you spend your days in the same way? If you cannot, how can you change Bill's schedule to make it a good schedule for you?

FIND THE MISSING WORDS

Each sentence tells one way to save time. Write each in your health notebook and fill in the missing words. The missing words are: *attention, right away, finish.*

1. When you have a study period in school, begin to study ——— ———.
2. If you have written work to do, ——— it in your study period so that you will not have to take it home.
3. Pay such good ——— in class that no ideas slip by you.

HOW TO BE FIT FOR WORK AND PLAY

TIRED MUSCLES

Open and shut one hand quickly a hundred times. Do you find this is easy to do for thirty to forty times and then does it become harder and harder? Do the muscles of your arm and hand ache? At last do you find you cannot go on opening and shutting your hand any longer?

Rest your hand and arm for ten minutes; then begin opening and shutting your hand again. Does the ache come sooner than before? If it does, the muscles are still tired.

What made the muscles get tired? Why does a person get tired after he has walked two or three miles?

It is because muscles at work, like engines at work, make a waste product. This waste product is like a poison to the muscles. It causes the muscles to become tired.

During rest, the waste product is carried away from the muscles. It is carried away by the blood, which is always moving through the body.

Perhaps you have felt stiff after some new kind of exercise. The stiffness, like the tired feeling, is caused by the waste product in the muscles. This stiffness may be prevented by a warm bath and a good rubbing all over with a rough towel. The bath and rubbing cause the blood to flow faster. When the blood flows faster, it removes the waste product faster.

PLANNING OUR EXERCISE AND REST

We should "work up" to any new kind of exercise. When the boys came to camp, the Big Chief let them take it easy for the first few days. There were no long hikes, no hard games, no races. This rule was made to keep the boys from getting all tired out the first few days. It gave them a chance to become used to the climate and to camp life.

At home, too, we should do any new kind of work or play only a little the first day, then a little more the second, and still more the third. That is one way of preventing stiff muscles.

On week ends and holidays we have to be careful not to overdo. When we overdo, we become overtired and our muscles feel stiff and sore.

Here is a rule about hiking: "Boys and girls

under twelve years old should not hike more miles in a day than the number of years old they are minus two." If you are ten years old, what is the longest hike you should take according to this rule?

Is this rule for boys and girls who are not used to taking walks? Is this rule for those who have just recovered from a serious illness or who are under the doctor's care? What rule should they follow?

Exercise and rest are somewhat like food. We need them every day. We need about the same amount of exercise and rest Monday at school, Saturday on a hike, or in summer at camp.

Outdoor play at recess uses different muscles

from work in class. It gives the other muscles a chance to rest. The muscles of the eyes get rest when we play out of doors.

If you eat lunch at school, you can rest by talking cheerfully or playing quiet games. If you eat lunch at home, you can lie down for a few minutes before starting back to school.

Outdoor work and play after school should be followed by rest before dinner or supper.

Did you ever hear of resting before you go to bed? That is not as silly as it sounds. A half hour's rest, reading a book, or listening to a quiet radio program helps you to get ready to sleep. It will keep you from being too tired to sleep.

Tired muscles are not the only reason for feeling tired. We soon get tired doing things we do not like to do. The way to prevent this kind of tiredness is to learn to like what we have to do and to have hobbies.

WHAT SLEEP DOES FOR YOU

Have you ever heard the saying, "Asleep at the switch"? If an engineer went to sleep at the switch—the place where trains are guided into the right tracks—many persons might be killed. Have you ever found yourself sleepy at the wrong time? Too little time in bed was probably the reason why.

Different persons need different amounts of sleep. A child needs more sleep than a grown person. He is growing as well as living. Growing children of your age should have about eleven hours of sleep each night.

The body builds itself up while you rest. During sleep it grows and stores up power for the next day's work and play. A person who has lost sleep often says, "I feel all worn out." Those words show just what has happened. The person's body has become worn out through loss of sleep.

Sleep helps to keep you good-natured and feeling that you are on top of the world. In an experiment * to find out facts about sleep, a number of boys and girls were allowed to stay up long past their regular bedtime. After a few days these children became so hard to live with—so cross and quarrelsome—that the experiment had to be stopped. After the children had gone back to their regular early bedtime, they became as good-natured as usual.

Sleep helps to keep you well. A person is more likely to catch colds and other diseases when he is overtired. Accidents also happen more frequently to people who are tired. Why should this be so?

Sleep helps you to do better schoolwork. If you are tired, it takes you longer to finish your lessons and you do not do them so well as when you are rested. Because you are sleepy, you read and write sleepily.

Sleep rests the body. It helps to prevent strain * on the heart * and other organs * of the body. If a person has one kind of heart trouble, the doctor

57

tells him to rest a great deal. Rest in bed is the best way to help cure a cold and other diseases. The person who can fall asleep quickly has a better chance of getting well quickly than the person who "just can't get to sleep."

MARY JANE'S BEDTIME

"I should not mind going to bed at eight o'clock if there were not so many interesting things to do," said Mary Jane one night as the clock struck eight. "I wish I could go to bed this minute," said her mother, "but I have a dozen things I must do before I can go to bed."

"I'm so tired I'd be glad to go to bed, but I must study for a test tomorrow," said Mary Jane's older sister. "You are lucky that you did your homework in school. Now you can go to bed at eight o'clock."

As Mary Jane put away the book she was reading, she thought, "Perhaps I am lucky to be able to go to bed at eight o'clock."

She said good night to everyone and went up to her bedroom. It was her own room. In it was her own bed with its firm mattress, small, flat pillow, and warm, clean, light covers.

After Mary Jane had cleaned her teeth and had taken a warm bath, she opened the window and turned out the light. There was no moon to look at tonight, but she saw the stars looking down at her in their friendly way and the old pine tree nodding its branches sleepily.

The room was dark and cool and quiet now. There was nothing more to do about today. Mary Jane stretched out comfortably and went right to sleep.

HOW TO GO TO SLEEP QUICKLY

When night falls on the earth, chickens and birds climb onto their roosts or into their nests and go to sleep. Many flowers fold up their petals.

Some people keep watch at night. Some people drive trains and boats through the darkness. But most people are fast asleep at night.

It is a good habit to fall asleep quickly. You should be asleep a few minutes after you have opened your window, turned out the light, and climbed into bed. In order to go to sleep quickly, you must relax. To relax is to feel like a rag doll, with no bones at all. If someone lifts your arm, it will drop back on the bed, just like a rag doll's. Your face is relaxed, and your knees are relaxed, too. You can make believe you are floating on a pink sunset cloud. You can take slow, deep breaths and make believe you are already asleep. That is a quick way to sail off into dreamland.

Donald could go to sleep any time of day or night.

He said: "You see, we kids can all go to sleep whenever we want to. Mother taught us how to relax when we were little."

There are two other ways to go to sleep quickly. One is to talk over with Mother or Father anything that has worried you during the day.

Another way is to drink no tea, coffee, or drinks that contain some of the kola nut. These drinks are stimulants.* They make it hard for you to relax and go to sleep.

Can You Answer, "Yes," to These Questions?

1. Can you relax and go to sleep quickly at any time of day or night?
2. Do you sleep alone or at least in a bed by yourself?
3. Do you use a low pillow?
4. Do you go to bed about the same time every night?
5. Do you eat a simple supper, with no tea or coffee?
6. Do you have light, warm, clean bed covers?
7. Do you sleep in a dark and quiet room?
8. Do you open the window to let in the cool, pleasant, fresh air?
9. Do you put the clothes you have worn during the day over a chair to air at night?
10. Do you wash your hands and face and clean your teeth before you go to bed?

Things to Do

1. Make a scrapbook of pictures of children getting ready to go to bed. Put in the scrapbook pictures of children sleeping in rooms that are just right for healthful sleep. Such pictures can be found in magazines, or you can draw them.

2. For one day watch a very young baby or a very young puppy or kitten. Do not disturb the baby or animal you watch. How much of the day does it sleep? Does it sleep long at one time or does it take a number of short naps?

3. Put a star on a calendar at home every day that you are in bed by eight o'clock.

4. Learn a song or poem about sleep to sing or tell to a younger brother or sister.

5. If you do not go to sleep quickly, read pages 60 and 61 again. What does it say may keep you wide awake? Try to find out what will help you best to go to sleep almost as soon as your head touches the pillow.

HOW TO HAVE STRENGTH TO WORK AND PLAY

HOW MUSCLES MOVE THE BODY

Without muscles you could not move unless you were carried by something or by someone. Every time you move by yourself, your muscles are working for you. When you raise your little finger, muscles move it. Muscles move your legs in walking and your arm in throwing a ball. In fact, some muscles are working whenever you move.

Feel the muscles in your arm. As you bend your arm at the elbow, you can feel the large muscle in the upper part of the arm thicken, shorten, and grow firmer. This muscle contracts.* By contracting, muscles can move any part of the body.

But, if muscles can do nothing but contract, how does your arm get straightened out again? After certain muscles have contracted, they may relax and let the part they act on fall back into its usual position. Or another set of muscles may pull the part back in place. We have two or more sets of muscles that act on each joint.* A joint is the place where one bone is joined to another, as at the elbow. One set of muscles in the arm contracts and bends the forearm toward the upper part of the arm. The other set contracts and straightens the arm again.

A muscle is usually largest in the middle and narrow at both ends. The middle is soft, like the red meat you see at the butcher's. The narrow ends, called tendons,* are smooth, white, and shiny.

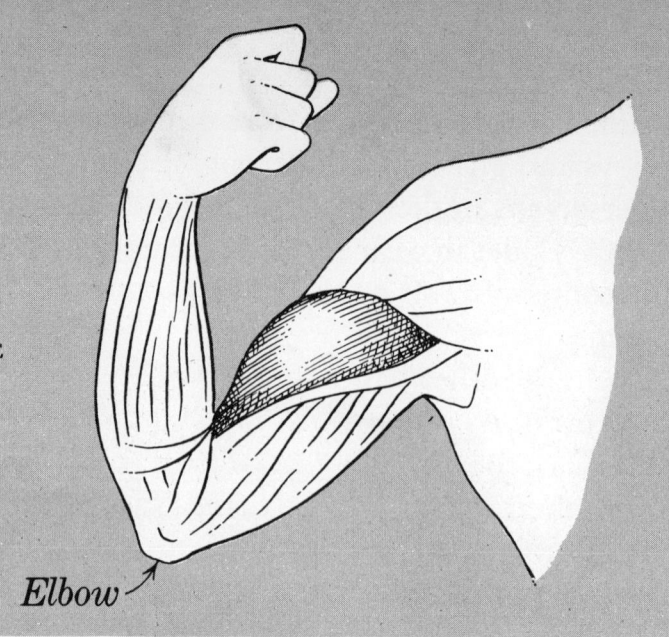

FIND THE LARGE MUSCLE IN THE ARM THAT IS CONTRACTED.

Elbow

They are very strong and can stand great strain. Tendons fasten the muscles to the bones. Bend your arm at the elbow to help you see how, when the muscle in the upper part of the arm contracts, its tendon moves the bone to which it is fastened.

You have 792 muscles. Many of these muscles work together to help you run and play games. They move your eyes when you read. They move your jaws when you chew. With the proper care muscles become stronger and work more smoothly. Unlike the engine which makes a car run, these muscles of yours do not wear out. They repair themselves if you give them the food and rest they need.

WHAT DO MUSCLES NEED?

Muscles need exercise. Working and playing help to make them firmer and stronger. Playing games and doing useful work out of doors help most boys and girls to build strong, useful muscles. If a person sits in the house all day and every day, if he always rides in a car instead of walking, his muscles become soft and weak. They become flabby,* not firm.

On the other hand, muscles must not be worked too hard. And they must not suddenly be made to do work they have not been used to doing. That is why the men on college teams "warm up" before beginning hard practice. "Warming up" means beginning to use your muscles in a certain way slowly and easily so that they will gradually get used to hard work.

The Big Chief at Bill's camp, you remember, always had the boys "work up" to new games and long hikes. Whenever they were learning to play a new game, they always began gradually. They would practice it for a short time the first day and then a longer time each day than the day before. In this way they learned to play many different games without getting stiff and sore while they were learning. At the end of the summer many of the boys could hike for eight miles or more without getting too tired and climb mountains without being lame the next day.

Besides exercise, muscles need oxygen.* Oxygen is the very breath of life. Every living thing must have it. Even a fire goes out if oxygen is taken away.

Try this experiment yourself. Take a small candle, like the candles that are used on birthday cakes. Heat the bottom to soften it and stick it onto a piece of wood. Then let it float in a dish of water. Light the candle and cover it with a glass, putting the edges of the glass under the water to keep air from getting to the candle. Notice what happens to the candle after a few minutes. Try to explain what happened. Remember that there is oxygen in the air all around us. Oxygen has no smell; and we cannot see it, because it has no color. Some of it is used up when anything burns.

Like the candle, muscles need oxygen in order to keep going. They get oxygen from the air we breathe in. The air passes down the throat and through a tube called the windpipe.* The windpipe is the pathway of the air into the lungs.* Find the nose in the drawing on page 69. Show how the air passes through the nose to the throat and down the windpipe to the air * sacs in the lungs.

But how does the oxygen get from the lungs to the muscles all over the body? Perhaps you will guess that the oxygen must be carried to the muscles by the blood. That is right. The oxygen passes through the very thin walls of the air sacs into the blood stream. Then it can be carried in the blood stream to the muscles.

As oxygen is taken up by the muscles, another gas called carbon* dioxide is given off. Carbon dioxide, too, is part of the air and is necessary for plants and animals. But the extra carbon dioxide

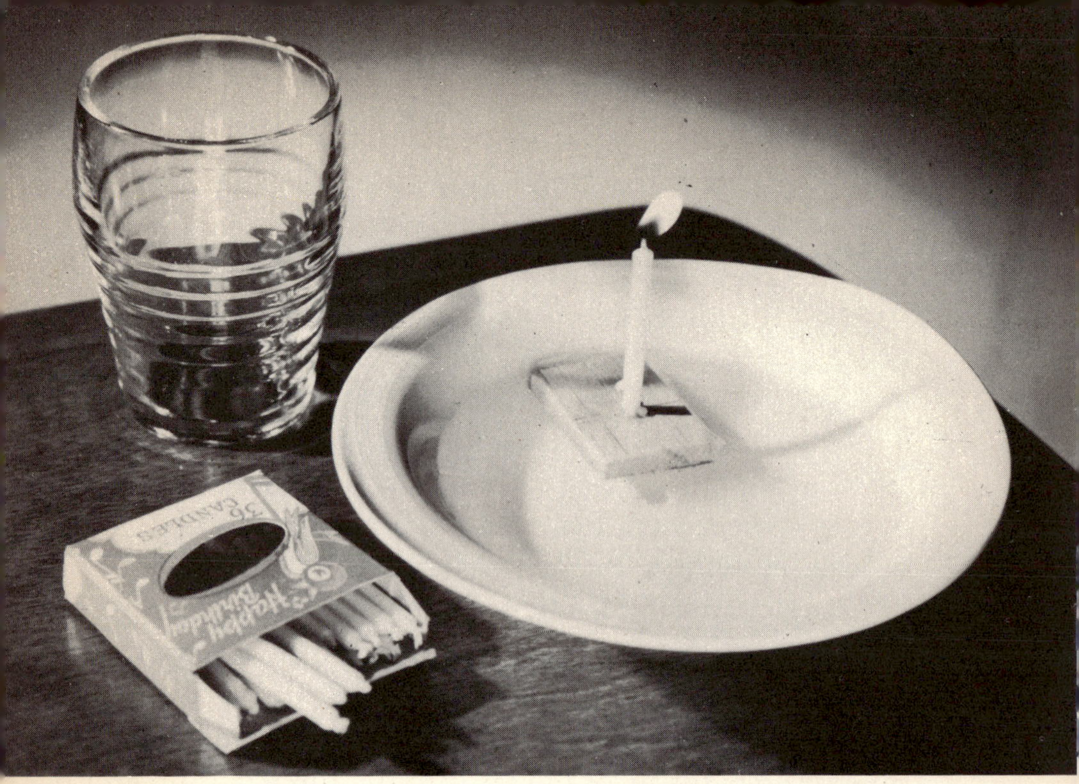
36 CANDLES
Happy Birthday

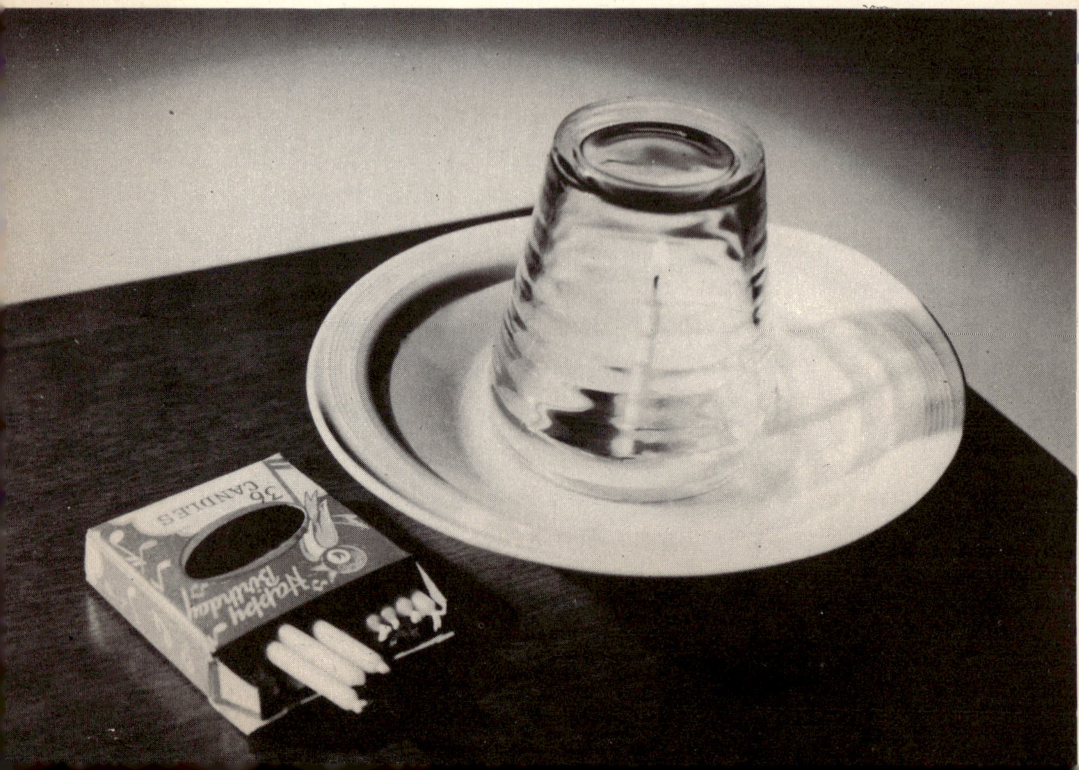
36 CANDLES
Happy Birthday

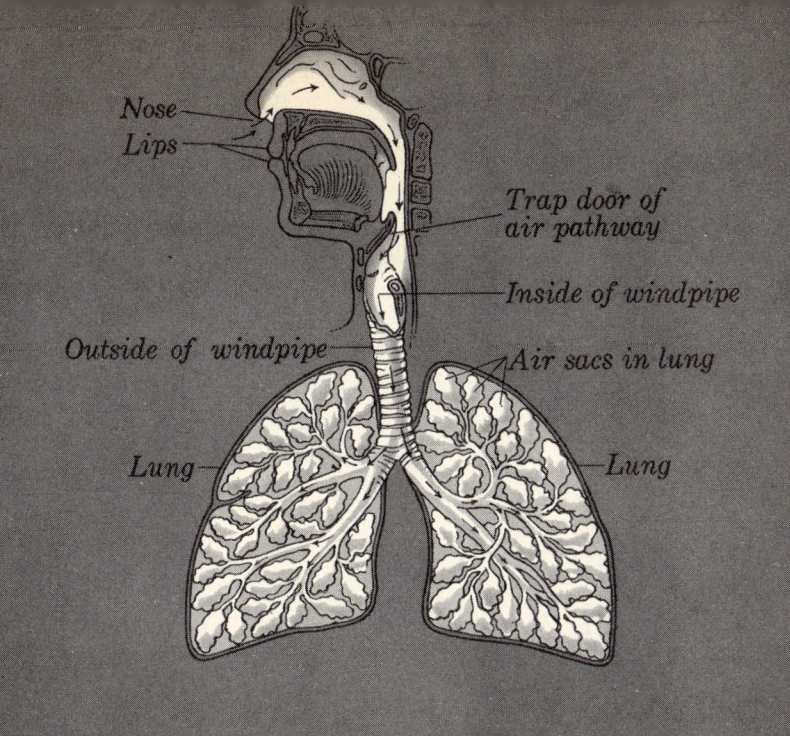

Nose
Lips
Trap door of air pathway
Inside of windpipe
Outside of windpipe
Air sacs in lung
Lung
Lung

that is given off must be carried out of the body. It is carried of course by the blood to the lungs. When you exhale,* or breathe out, the lungs send carbon dioxide up through the windpipe and out through the nose. You breathe out more carbon dioxide than you inhale,* or breathe in.

The air that you breathe out into a room can easily be exchanged for fresh air. If you open the windows top and bottom, the cool, fresh air can come in at the bottom and the warmer, used air can go out at the top. Do you know why the air moves in this way? The air you breathe out is warmer than the fresh air that comes into the room. Warm air is lighter; it goes up. Cold air is heavier;

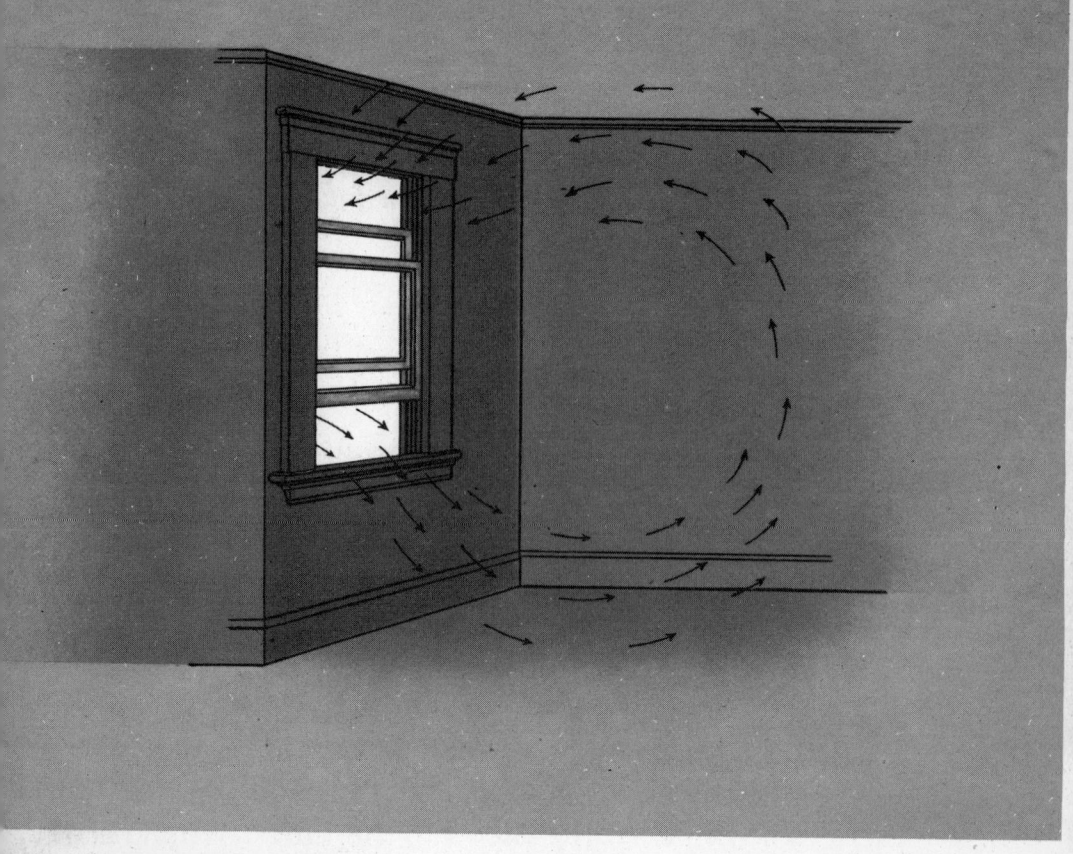

it sinks. So, when you have the windows open at the top and at the bottom, the air will move gently through the room.

In most rooms there is plenty of oxygen. The muscles can easily get as much as they need.

Besides oxygen and the right kind of exercise, muscles need food. But no one food is a special muscle-building food. All the good foods are good "muscle foods"—milk, bread or cereal, fruits and vegetables, eggs, and meat or fish. These foods help to build strong muscles and to give you power to work and play.

Questions to Answer

1. What is it that moves any part of your body?
2. How does your arm get straightened out again after you have bent it to "show your muscle"?
3. How do muscles move bones?
4. Name one way in which muscles are like an engine in an automobile. Name one way in which they are different.
5. Why did the Big Chief at Bill's camp want the boys to play a new game for only a short time at the beginning?
6. What do college boys on teams mean when they talk of "warming up" before a game?
7. What three things do muscles need? How can you give them these three things?

Can You Answer, "Yes," to These Questions?

1. Do you practice each new kind of game or exercise only a short time at first?
2. Do you have fresh air in your rooms?
3. Do you try to keep your rooms at a temperature of about 68°?

Things to Do

1. Where do you play? Is your playground a pleasant and safe place? If there is no place but the street where you can play, ask your parents and teachers to help you and the other boys and girls to find or make a playground. In the city you may have a part of one street shut off at certain hours, so that automobiles and wagons cannot pass through. Do you know of any streets near your home that are shut off to make play streets some of the time?
2. Find work that you can do to help your father and mother. Useful outdoor work is good exercise. Ask your

father and mother to set certain times by the clock when you will work for them. In the country your work may be pulling weeds, hoeing, feeding chickens, looking for eggs, or cutting wood. In the city it may be going to the store, taking your baby brother or sister for a walk, hanging out clothes, or sweeping the walk.

3. Get two boxes. Into one put things with which to play on sunshiny days, such as balls, ropes, and a kite. Into the other box put playthings for rainy days, when you want to stay indoors part of the time. Picture puzzles, other puzzles, paints and crayons, and clothes to dress up in for plays make fun for rainy days.

4. Read again pages 49 to 52. Write a story telling how you planned your days better. Did you find time for outdoor fun and did you also allow time for all the rest and sleep you need?

Unit IV

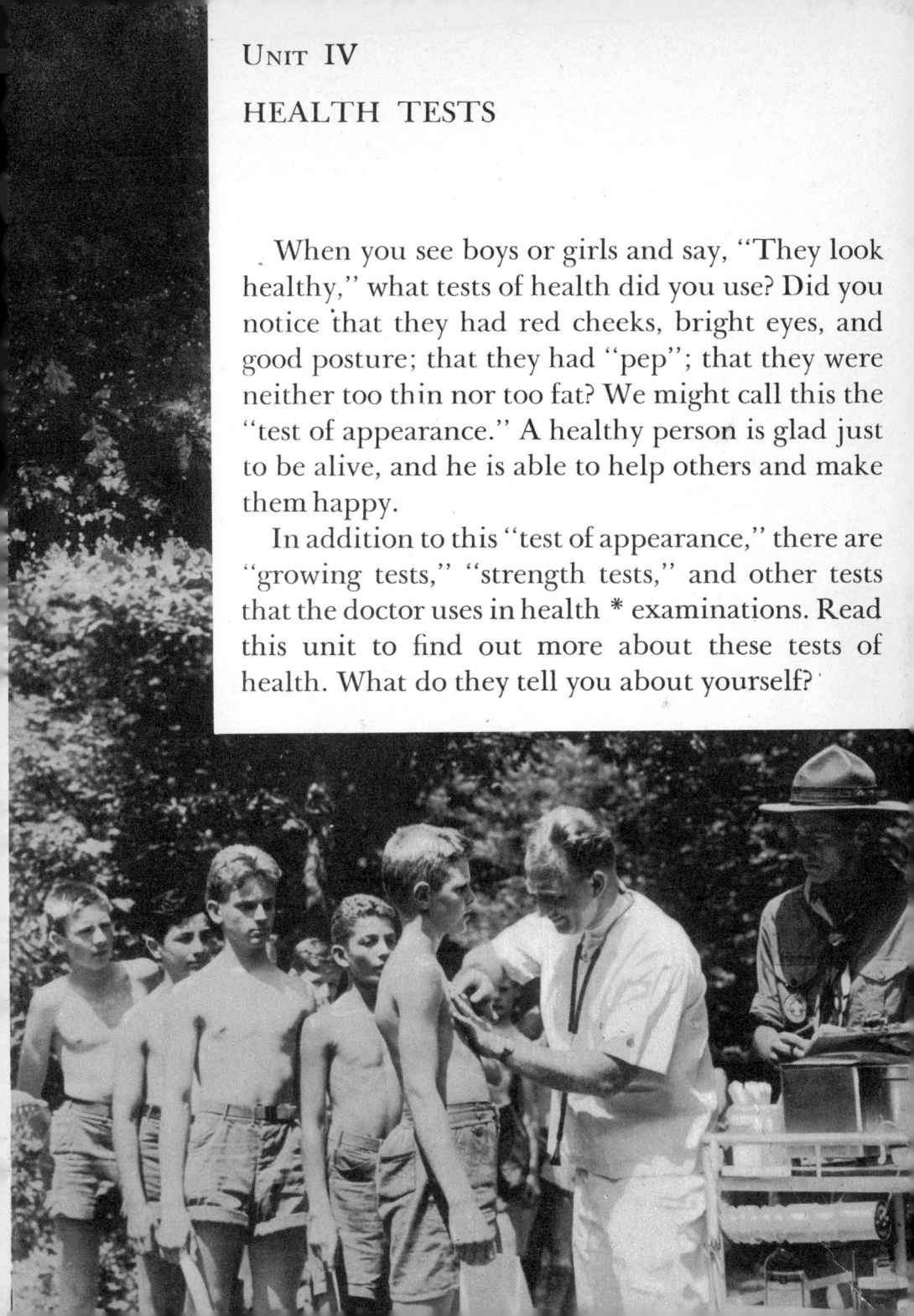

HEALTH TESTS

When you see boys or girls and say, "They look healthy," what tests of health did you use? Did you notice that they had red cheeks, bright eyes, and good posture; that they had "pep"; that they were neither too thin nor too fat? We might call this the "test of appearance." A healthy person is glad just to be alive, and he is able to help others and make them happy.

In addition to this "test of appearance," there are "growing tests," "strength tests," and other tests that the doctor uses in health * examinations. Read this unit to find out more about these tests of health. What do they tell you about yourself?

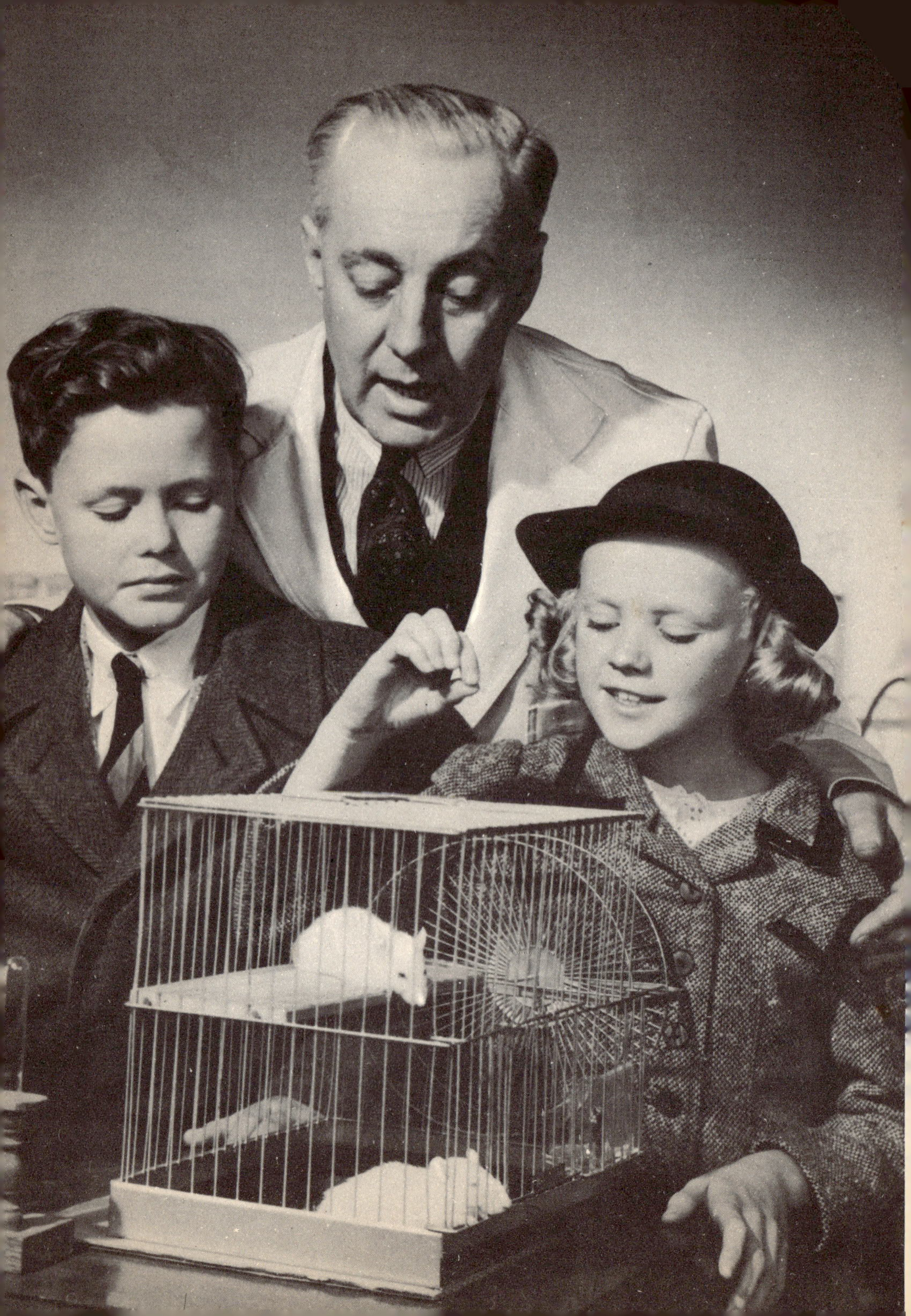

THE GROWING TEST

Every young living thing grows. Kittens grow on milk. Chickens grow on grain and grass. Rabbits grow on green plants, carrots, and other vegetables. Babies grow on milk. Boys and girls grow on milk, grains, fruit and vegetables, butter, meat, and eggs.

Pictures of yourself, taken since you were a baby, placed side by side show how much you have grown. Gain in height and weight is one test of health.

HELPS IN GROWING

One day Jim and his sister Helen went to see their Uncle Charlie. They found him at work in his laboratory * on the top floor of a tall building. Uncle Charlie was trying to find out what foods make animals grow best. He called this "making experiments" or "doing experimental work."

He was putting a big white rat on a scale. The rat sat very quietly. Uncle Charlie read its weight and wrote it on a card.

"Why are you weighing the rat so carefully?" Jim asked.

"Weighing the rat is part of one of my experiments," said Uncle Charlie. "I'm trying to discover the most healthful foods. The foods that make animals grow also make children grow. And gaining weight is one of the signs of health in young rats as well as in boys and girls."

"What thick, soft fur the young rat has! How bright his pink eyes are!" said Helen.

"How lively he is!" exclaimed Jim.

"You see signs of a healthy rat," said Uncle Charlie.

"What does he eat?" asked Helen.

"This rat has always had whole milk and whole-wheat bread to eat. He has shown a gain in weight every time I've weighed him. Look at his card."

Helen and Jim read the figures on the weight card. Sure enough, every week the rat had gained in weight.

"Rats that are fed on whole milk and whole-wheat bread gain in weight as this rat did. Now look at this rat," said Uncle Charlie, taking a small rat out of another cage.

"Why, he's just a young rat," said Jim. "Is the other one his mother?"

"It looks that way, doesn't it? You'll be surprised when I tell you that the big rat and the little rat are twins."

"Twins!" exclaimed Jim. "Then they were born at the same time."

"Yes, they were born at the same time. At the beginning of the experiment both weighed exactly the same. Look at the figures on the two cards."

Jim looked at the two cards. For several weeks both rats gained in weight. Then one stopped growing. Next he began to lose weight.

"What made the difference?" asked Jim.

76

"Food made the difference," said Uncle Charlie.

"The little rat had nothing but white bread and meat, while the big rat had whole milk and whole wheat."

When Jim and Helen went home, they told their mother about Uncle Charlie's experiment. "Food makes a great difference in health and growth," they said. "Uncle Charlie's experiments with white rats prove it."

During the World Wars many children did not have enough food. Some of them stopped growing. When the wars were over and these children were given the right kind and amount of food, they grew again. But they did not grow as tall as they would have grown, and their bones were not so well shaped.

But we must remember that gaining weight is only one sign of health in young children. A small, thin child is not always unhealthy. He may feel as well and lively as the bigger boys and girls. Each child should grow in his own best way.

Food is not the only thing that makes a difference in children's health and growth.

Sunlight makes a difference.

The right kind of excrcise makes a difference.

Sleep and rest make a difference.

Being happy and loved makes a difference.

Having no serious defects * makes a difference.

If you do not grow for three months, ask your doctor what is best for you to do.

DO YOU WANT TO CHANGE YOUR WEIGHT?

If you are too thin and wish to gain in weight, you can do these things:

1. Drink a glass of milk at every meal. Drink another glass at your regular midmorning lunch if you feel hungry. Milk is a food, not just something to drink.

2. Eat vegetables or fruit at every meal and an apple, orange, tomato, or other fruit for your after-school lunch.

3. Eat a good breakfast every morning. Children who want to gain weight drink a glass of orange juice or tomato juice when they get up. Then at breakfast time they may have a cup of cooked cereal with cream, an egg on buttered toast, a glass of milk or a cup of hot milk flavored with cocoa or some other flavor, and more toast and butter if they feel hungry.

4. Eat slowly and talk about pleasant things. Food does us more good if we are happy at mealtime.

5. Play or walk or sit in the sunshine part of every day—at recess, at noon, and as soon as school is out.

6. Rest lying down during the day. Shut your eyes and relax. Make the muscles in your arms and legs feel loose, like a rag doll's arms and legs. Then you will have a real rest. Do quiet things part of the time.

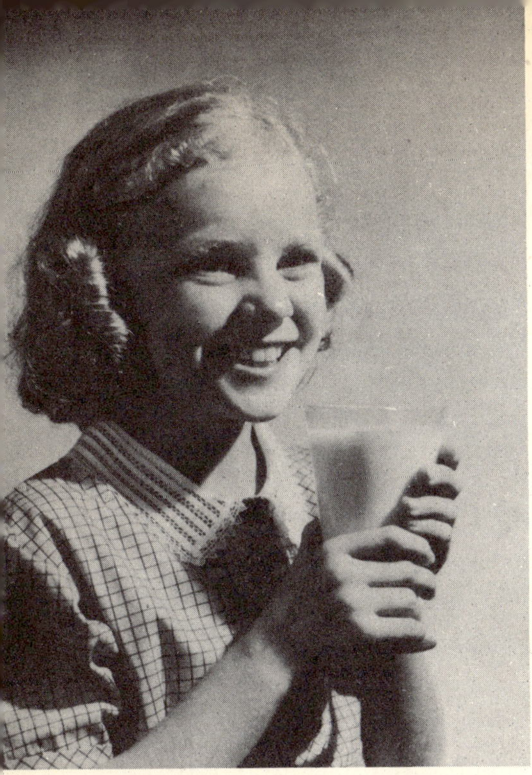
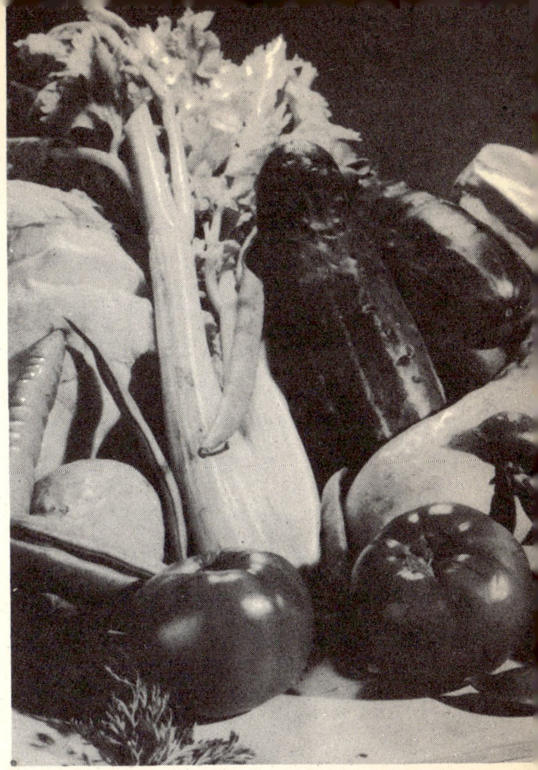
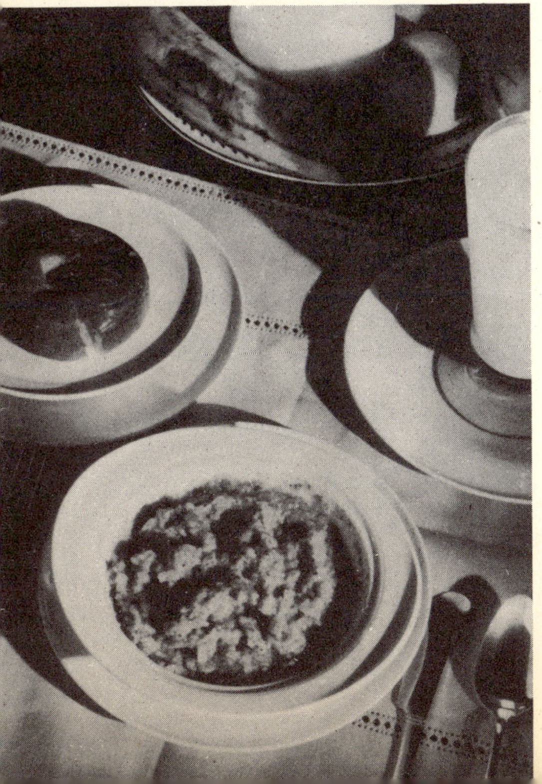
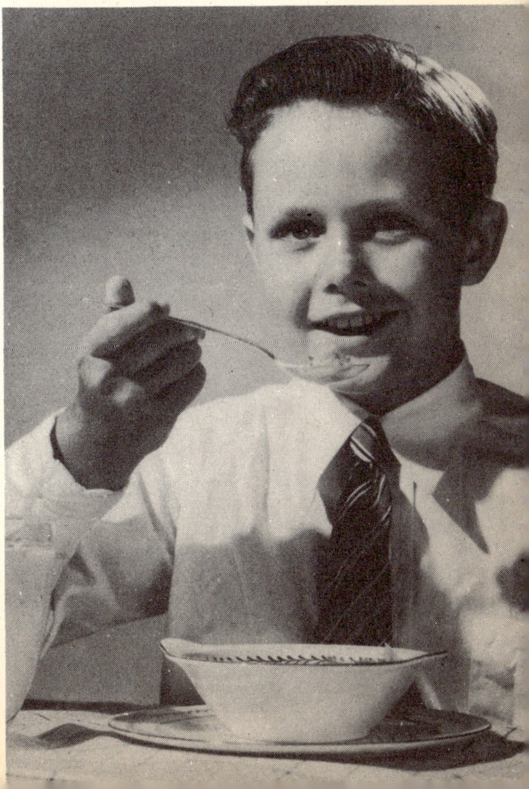

7. Sleep eleven hours at night. While you are resting and sleeping, the body has the best chance to use some of the food for growth.

8. Have a yearly health examination to make sure that there is no special reason why you are not gaining in weight. If something seems to be keeping you from growing, find out from the doctor what to do.

If you are too fat, you can follow every rule given for thin children except one. That one rule is not to eat as much as the thin child. You do not need a midmorning lunch or as much bread and butter. You should eat fruit instead of cake and candy.

Other Children's Questions

Answer these questions, which other children have asked about gaining weight. If you do not know the right answer to a question, find it in the pages you have just read.

1. How can I gain in weight?
2. What is a good breakfast to help me gain weight?

Find the Right Word

Here is a list of words. Choose the right words for the blanks in the following sentences. The missing words are: vegetables, muscles, whole milk, meat, exercise, sleep. (Do not write in this book.)

1. The rat that gained in weight was fed on ——— and whole-wheat bread.
2. The rat that did not make a good gain in weight was fed on white bread and ———.
3. Sunlight, rest, sleep, ———, and food help children to grow well and strong.

4. One sign of good health is firm ———.
5. Every day we need some ——— and fruit.
6. A thin child needs plenty of ——— and rest.

Things to Think About

1. Why are the right kind and amount of food important? Can a thin child eat too much?
2. How can you tell a healthy boy or girl?

Things to Do

1. Find the pictures on page 79 to match some of the rules for gaining weight given on pages 78 and 80.
2. Get weighed every month. Keep a record like the one below to see how many pounds you gain month by month. If you do not gain for three months, ask the doctor to help you find the reason why. Do everything that he tells you to do and watch your weight during the next months.

	Sept.	Oct.	Nov.	Dec.	Jan.	Feb.	Mar.	Apr.	May	June
Height in inches	54	54								
Weight in pounds	70	70½								
Gain in pounds										
Loss in pounds										

3. If you do not like milk or green vegetables, learn to like them. One schoolboy said, "I think it is just a notion when we don't like this and don't like that." If you do not like the taste of milk, add a little chocolate or other flavor that you do like. Use milk in soups, in cup custard, in rice pudding, and in other dishes that you like. If you do not like lettuce, ask your mother to let you have it in a salad with oranges or other food you like. If you do not like spinach or cabbage, ask your mother to cook it or let you

81

cook it with the cover off the pot and just long enough to become tender. Then the spinach or the cabbage will be green and good and you will like it.

4. Go to the county fair if you have a chance. Ask the men and boys who own the prize pigs and cows and sheep and chickens to tell you what makes these prize animals so big and healthy.

5. Make a vegetable book, using one page for each kind of vegetable. All vegetables are parts of plants. They are the parts where the plants have stored the most food. That is why these parts make good food for us. These are the kinds of vegetables:

    (1) Roots of plants—carrots
        Name another root vegetable.
    (2) Underground stems of plants—potatoes
        Name another underground stem vegetable.
    (3) Buds of plants—asparagus tips
        Name another bud vegetable.

(4) Leaves of plants—spinach
   Name another leaf vegetable.
(5) Flowers of plants—cauliflower
   Name another flower vegetable.
(6) Seeds of plants—peas
   Name another seed vegetable.

Find or draw pictures of all these vegetables for the class vegetable book or your own health notebook.

THE DOCTOR'S TESTS

In a health examination you take many health tests. The doctor tests the health of the eyes and ears, the nose and throat, the heart and lungs. He notes tooth defects. He checks up on posture and health habits. In this way he can tell you when you are in good health. If you are not, he can find the defects that keep you from being in the best of health.

Jane's school had had no nurse and no doctor for many years. But one year the parents said: "We must have a doctor in our school. We must also have a nurse." They decided to have Dr. White visit the school and give health examinations. Then they paid Miss Stevens, who was a nurse, to stay all day in the school.

One of the first things Dr. White and Miss Stevens did was to give every child a health examination. Jane wondered what a health examination was. She found out when her turn came.

Her mother was invited to come to Jane's health examination. She came, because she wanted to hear what the doctor would say about Jane's health. The school nurse was also present. She said: "We are glad your mother came. We wish all the mothers could come when their boys and girls have health examinations."

CARE OF THE EYES

The nurse weighed and measured Jane and helped to test her eyes and ears. Jane passed the tests. Although she had no eye defects, she wanted to know how to take good care of her eyes. The nurse told Jane these important things to do:

1. Sit so that the light shines on your book, not in your eyes.

2. Hold your book up about a foot from your eyes.

3. Read in a good, steady light, not too dim and not so bright that it hurts.

4. Use your eyes, rest your eyes, use your eyes.

The eyes are moved by six pairs of very small muscles. After you have been using these small muscles in reading and writing, rest them. One way to rest them is by looking out at the sky or some other far-away place. Another way to rest the eye muscles is to play out of doors. Change from one thing to another like this:

Reading	Playing ball
Playing running games .	Sewing
Playing the piano	Skating

In this way you will rest your eye muscles and exercise your big muscles.

5. Keep your fingers away from your eyes. Use only your own washcloth and towel—never anyone else's.

6. If something flies into your eye, never rub the eye. If the speck does not come out soon, find a nurse or doctor to take it out.

7. Have an eye examination at least every two years.

A QUICK, NEW EYE EXAMINATION

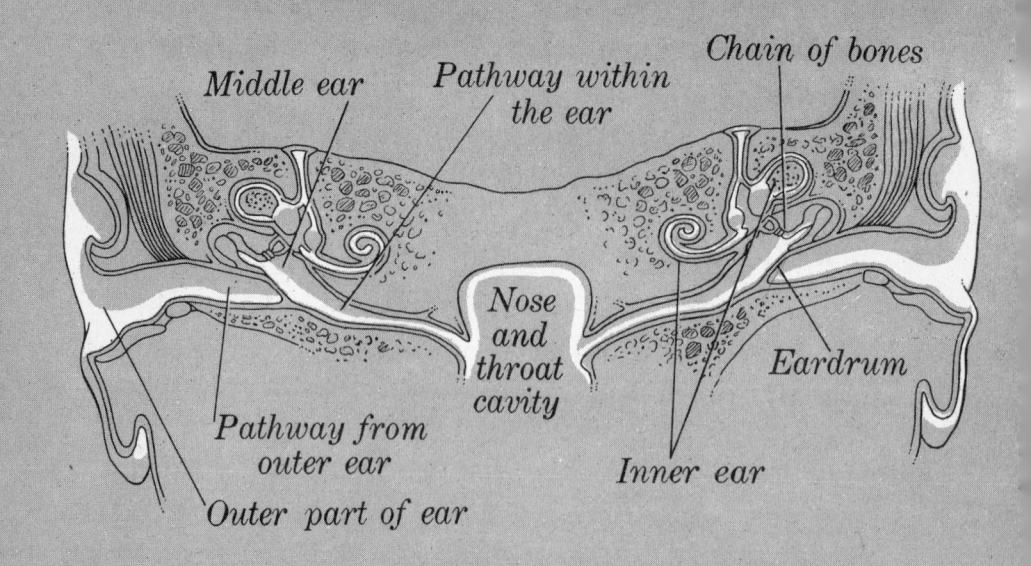

Middle ear — *Pathway within the ear* — *Chain of bones* — *Eardrum* — *Inner ear* — *Nose and throat cavity* — *Pathway from outer ear* — *Outer part of ear*

THE EARS AND THEIR CARE

Jane had already learned that the outer part of the ears—the part you see—catches sounds in somewhat the same way that the mouthpiece of a telephone does. The sound travels along a tube to the eardrum.* Beyond the eardrum is a chain of three small bones, which make the sound louder and pass it on to the inner part of the ear. From this hidden inner part of the ear the sound is carried by nerves * to the brain.* You do not hear any sound until it has reached Central, the brain.

Another pathway leads from the middle part of the ear to the nose and throat. Germs that may cause a cold or sore throat sometimes creep along this tube to the ear. Then a doctor is needed. An earache says:

86

"Your ears need help; they're very sick.
Send for the doctor, quick, quick, quick."

"You have good ears, Jane," said Miss Stevens. "Take care of them. Do all you can to prevent colds. If any small, sharp, or hard object gets in your ear, have a doctor take it out. Such objects can break the eardrum and cause deafness. Always wash your ears gently with clean, warm water and a soft cloth. Holding the cloth over the end of your finger is the best way to use it. People should never hit others on the ears or make very loud sounds close to them. To do so may hurt the eardrums."

"I never thought about taking care of my ears before," said Jane. "Now that I know, I'll be careful not to hurt my ears or other people's ears either. We get second teeth, but we never get second ears."

ATTENTION TO THE TEETH

Dr. White found that some of Jane's teeth needed attention. He told her mother that she should take Jane to the dentist at once and have her teeth cared for.

EXAMINATION OF NOSE, THROAT, AND LUNGS

Dr. White looked in Jane's nose and throat. Near the two openings of the nose are little hairs, which help to catch the dust in the air. The lining of the nose is wet, and that also helps to keep dust from going down into the lungs. The inside of the nose is warm, too. It warms cold air before letting it into the lungs.

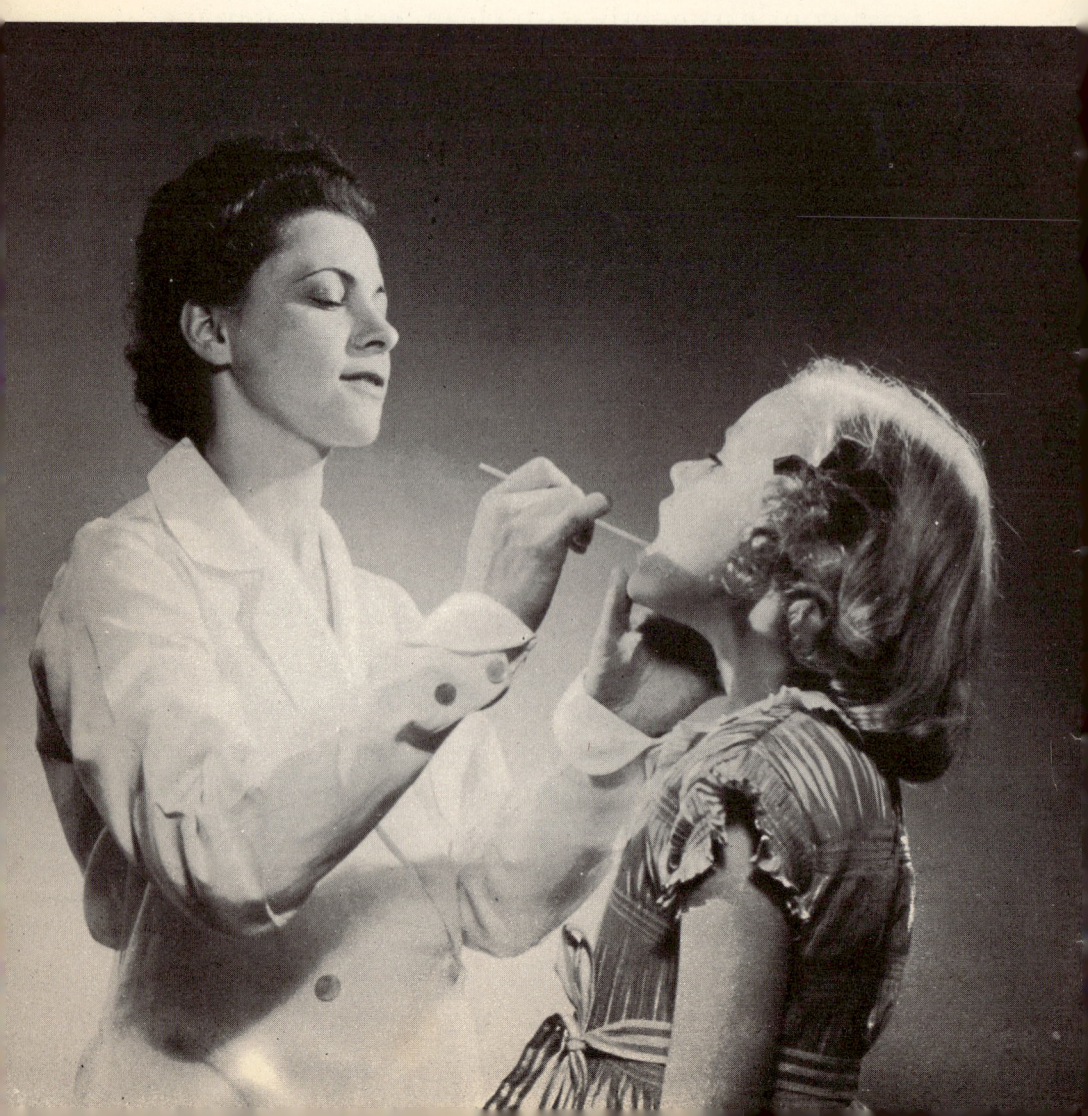

Sometimes the pathway through the nose and throat is stopped up by adenoids or adenoid tissue * growing back of the nose or in the throat. If that happens, the air has to enter through the mouth. The mouth cannot warm and clean the air so well as the nose. So cold, dusty air goes from the mouth down the windpipe into the lungs.

If you take a mirror to look at your throat, perhaps you can see your tonsils. They are two small lumps of tissue, one on each side of your throat. If you cannot see them, you may have had them taken out when you were very young.

"You do not have adenoids," Dr. White told Jane. "So you do not have to breathe through your mouth."

"Suppose I had adenoids?" Jane asked.

"Then you would probably catch cold more easily," replied Dr. White. "Adenoids and tonsils that have nests of germs in them would have to be taken out, for good health's sake."

"My little brother still has his tonsils. Perhaps they have nests of germs in them. He has a sore throat often. Sometimes his hands and knees hurt," said Jane.

"A doctor should look at his throat," said Dr. White. "Sore throats may lead to a very dangerous disease, rheumatic * fever."

"Is it a common disease?" asked Jane.

"Yes, it is," said Dr. White, "especially among children your age or younger. Rheumatic fever is a great enemy of childhood. People used to say that children had 'growing pains.' That is a mistake. Growing is painless.

"Whenever children have pains in any joint, they should be taken to a doctor. Sore throats should be watched. If a child has rheumatic fever, it can now be cured."

Dr. White found nothing wrong with Jane's lungs, but he said, "Have them X-rayed * later."

THE HEART EXAMINATION

Next Dr. White examined Jane's heart. The heart is close to the lungs. You have probably felt it beating hard when you have been running fast.

The heart keeps the blood moving through the body. In one way it is like a pump. At each beat blood is pushed out of the heart into the blood * vessels. Then the blood vessels carry the blood to all

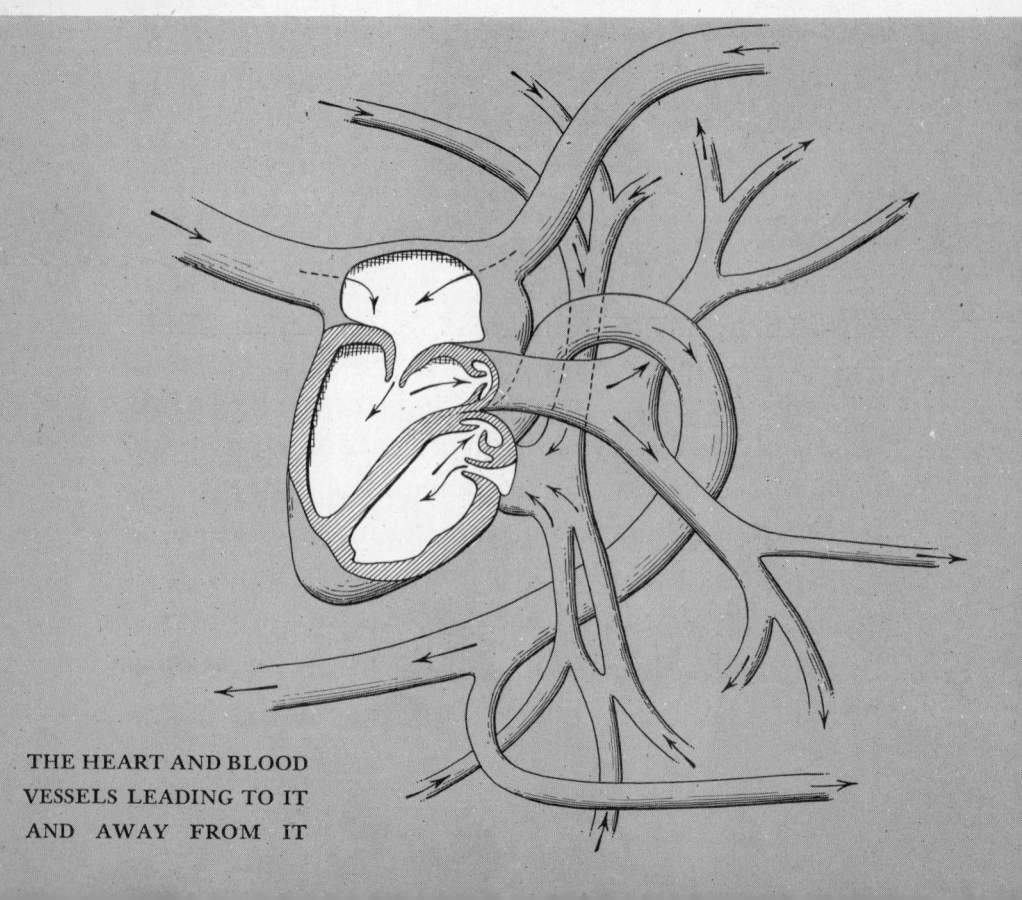

THE HEART AND BLOOD VESSELS LEADING TO IT AND AWAY FROM IT

parts of the body and back again to the heart. Round and round the blood flows. It circulates.* It carries food and oxygen to all parts of the body. It carries waste away from all parts of the body.

Dr. White found nothing wrong with Jane's heart. But he told her she should have her heart tested after any disease such as scarlet fever or measles. The reason for this is that some diseases hurt the heart; but, if the right care is taken at once, the heart can grow strong again.

A TEST OF POSTURE

Next the doctor looked at the way Jane stood. He gave her an *A* for very good posture. The *A* meant that Jane was standing well. She held in her abdomen * and chin. That kept her chest and the top of her head up high. She felt comfortable standing this way.

THE TEST OF HEALTH HABITS

Last of all, Dr. White asked Jane about her health habits. He told her to be sure to remember to drink a glass of milk at every meal, to eat some raw vegetable or fruit daily, and to play out of doors at least two hours every day. Jane and her mother promised to do everything the doctor told them to do.

A health examination every year helps a person to keep well and strong. After the doctor tells us what to do, the rest is up to us.

Yes or No?

1. A dim light is the best light to use in reading.
2. Outdoor play and plenty of sleep have nothing to do with good eyes.
3. Germs cannot pass from the throat to the eardrum.
4. If something gets in an ear, a doctor should take it out.
5. Adenoids make you breathe through your mouth.
6. Tonsils that are diseased should be taken out.
7. It is wise to have a health examination every year.

Things to Think About

1. "A stitch in time saves nine." Tell, in your own words, what this old saying means. In what ways is a health examination "a stitch in time"?
2. In what ways are your ears like a telephone? Draw the parts of this telephone line of yours.

Things to Do

1. Ask your mother and father to let you read parts of this unit to them.
2. Look at your hands and nails. Look at yourself in the looking glass. Do you pass these tests of appearance? Are you as neat and clean as you would like to be? What can you do tonight and tomorrow morning so that you will come to school so clean and neat that the class will be proud of you?
3. Check yourself right this minute. Are you holding this book about a foot from your eyes? Is a good light falling on your book from above and behind you? Think of these questions every time you sit down to read.
4. Which of the health habits mentioned in this unit have you formed? Which do you need to work on?
5. Add the new health words in this unit to your dictionary, as you have done before.

UNIT V

MORE WAYS TO KEEP WELL

Scientists have helped people keep well by making discoveries. Doctors tell us about these discoveries and show us how they help us to prevent illness.

Have you had to miss good times because you were sick? Could your illness have been prevented? Is keeping well your problem? Or the doctor's? Or your mother and father's? Or everybody's problem? What can you do to keep well?

What can you do to help others to keep well?

Read this unit to find out how good teeth help to keep you well and how to prevent some dangerous diseases that were once common.

You will find some new words in this unit. Perhaps you will ask a doctor or nurse to tell you more about them.

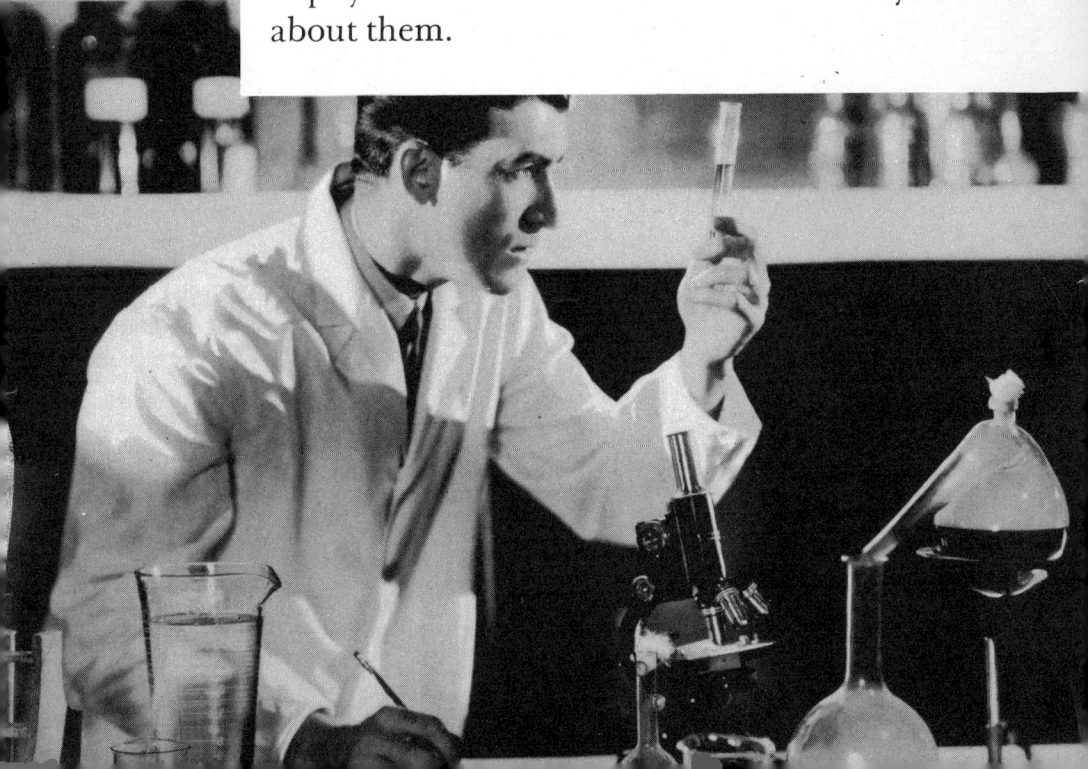

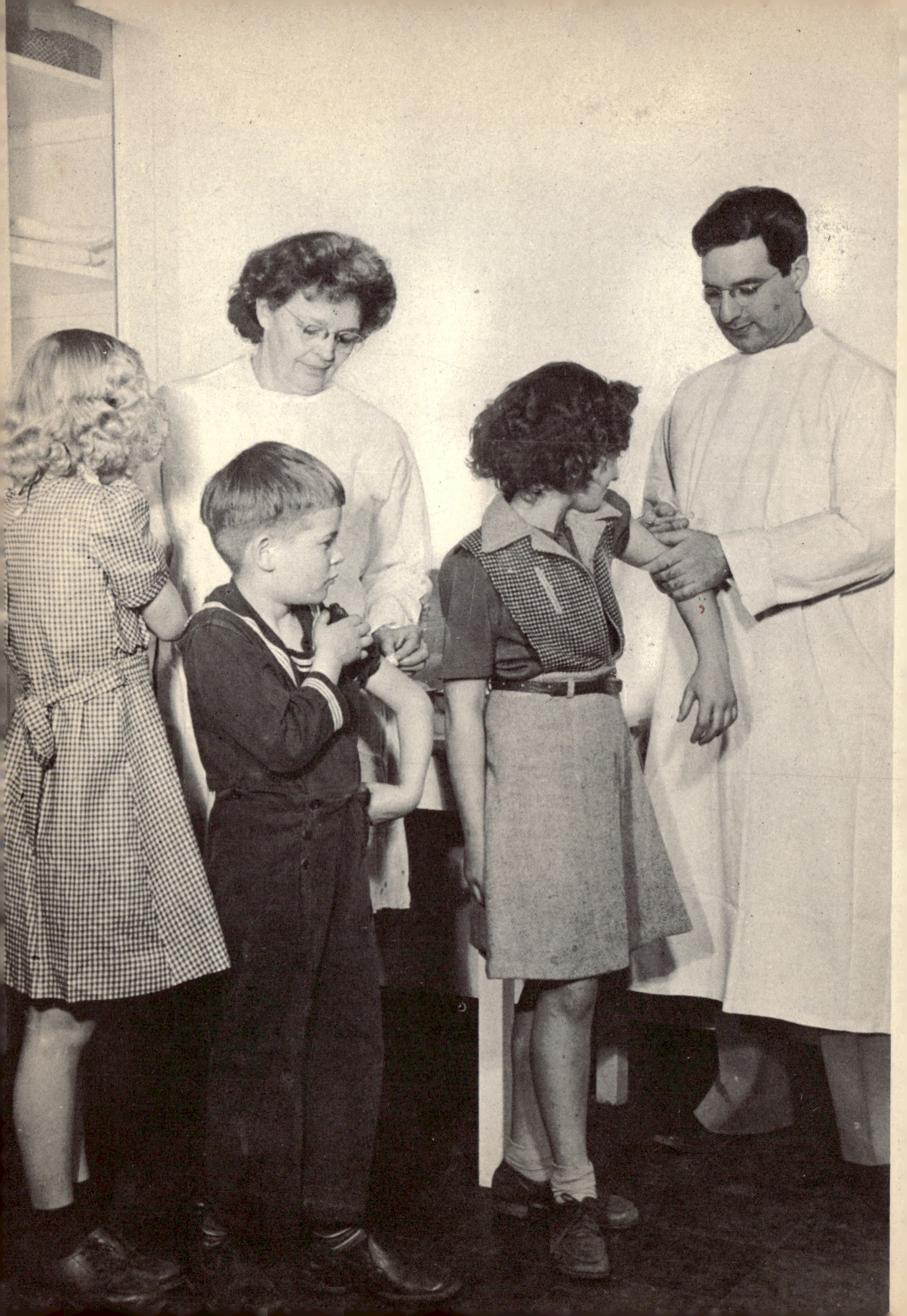

VISITING THE DENTIST

We call our first teeth "baby teeth," because we are very young when they come in. Later we get a new set of teeth. If we take care of this second set, they are more likely to last the rest of our lives. We shall not need a third set, as Mary's grandfather did. Of course there is just one way to get a third set, and you know what that is.

Jean had a toothache. It had kept her awake the night before long after eight o'clock, the time when she was usually asleep. Her mother took her to the dentist's the first thing in the morning.

"Is the pain acute*?" the dentist asked.

Jean looked puzzled.

"*Acute* means *sharp*," explained her mother. "An acute pain means a sharp pain."

"Oh," said Jean, "I surely think this toothache is acute. What makes it acute?"

The dentist examined her tooth.

"You have a large cavity * in the second tooth from the center in the upper jaw," he told her.

He carefully cleaned the cavity in Jean's tooth. Cleaning it hurt her, but she sat still and held her mouth open so that the dentist could get the cavity cleaned quickly. Then he filled it.

"How did that cavity get so large?" Jean asked.

"If I'm going to answer that question, I'll have to tell you how teeth are built," the dentist said. "The teeth, as you know, are hard, like bone. Each tooth has three parts—the crown,* the neck,* and the root.* The part you see above the gum is the crown. The part that is under the gum is the root. The part between the crown and the root is the neck. Find the crown and the neck of one of your own teeth."

Jean pointed to the crown and the neck of one of her teeth and to the root, hidden by the gum.

"The hard, white material covering the crown is called *enamel*,*" the dentist continued. "It is built of very small blocks. The teeth are not enamel all the way through.

"Under the enamel is a substance called *dentine*.* It is softer than the enamel. For that reason decay* works its way more quickly through the dentine than through the enamel. The dentine contains tiny tubes which carry food to the enamel.

"In the center of the tooth is an open space, which is the supply house of the tooth. It contains many blood vessels that bring food to the tooth. This food is sent to the parts of the tooth that need to be built up. In this supply house there are also nerves, which carry messages to and from the tooth. It is the nerves that carry the sad news of a toothache. The blood vessels and nerves enter each tooth through a hole in the root.

"Now you can see how the cavity in your tooth grew so large. The tooth may have been poorly built in the first place.

"One of the little blocks of hard enamel may have been chipped or cracked. Perhaps you used your teeth as a nutcracker, or perhaps you crunched hard candy.

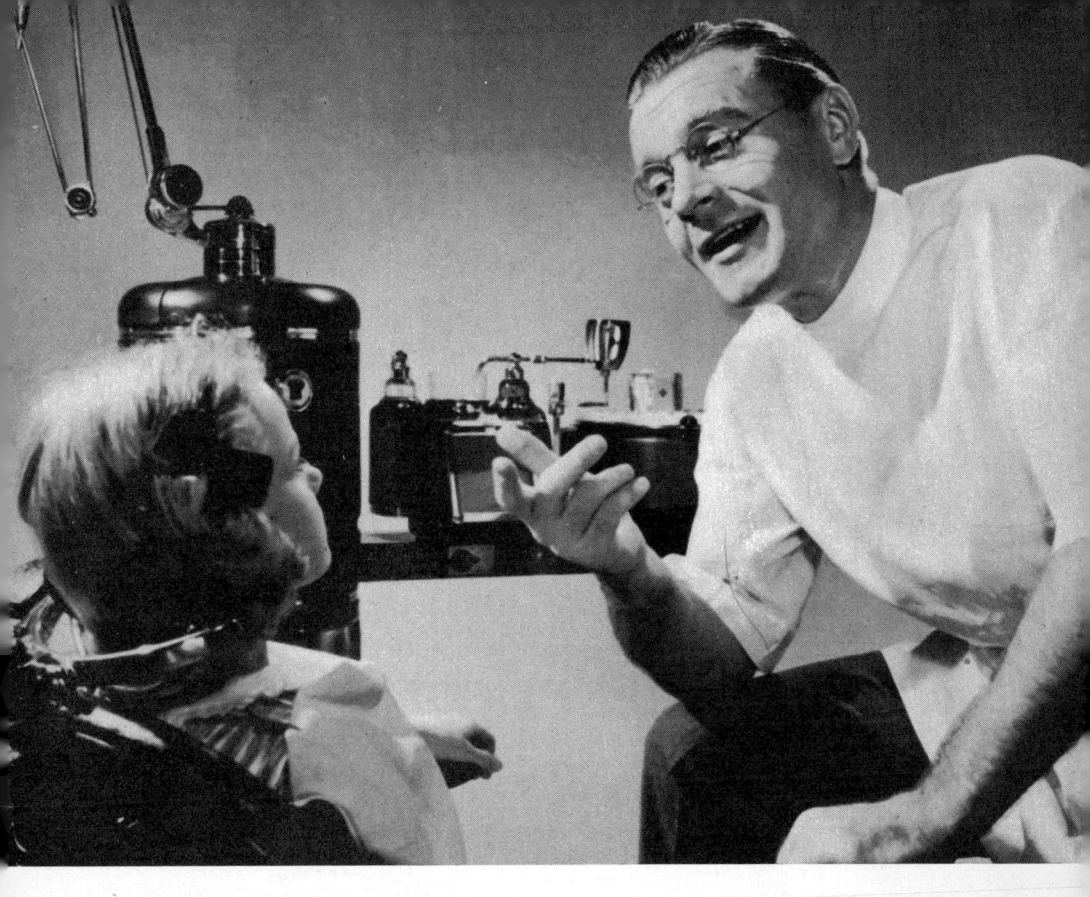

"Acids * used in making soft drinks (not fresh fruit juice) may harm the teeth. There are bacteria, too, that cause some foods to form acids. These acids eat their way slowly through the enamel to the dentine. The dentine begins to decay. The cavity grows larger. The decay may even reach the center of the tooth unless the hole is filled.

" 'A stitch in time saves nine,' you know. Filling the hole when it is small may save a tooth. If you had had a dental * examination twice a year, the cavity in that tooth would not have had a chance to grow so large."

"And if you had cleaned each tooth more thoroughly," Jean's mother said.

"But not scrubbed back and forth at the edge of the gums. Such scrubbing wears away the thin enamel," added the dentist. "Dental * floss, used carefully, is a fine way to clean between the teeth.

"Food that requires thorough chewing instead of only soft, sweet food helps to prevent decay. Raw carrots, celery, cabbage, apples, and hard toast and rolls are good foods to clean the teeth. They also help to make healthy gums," said the dentist.

"All good foods feed the teeth. Choose milk, tomato juice, orange juice, and lettuce often. Sunlight and the vitamins in fish-liver oil help the body to

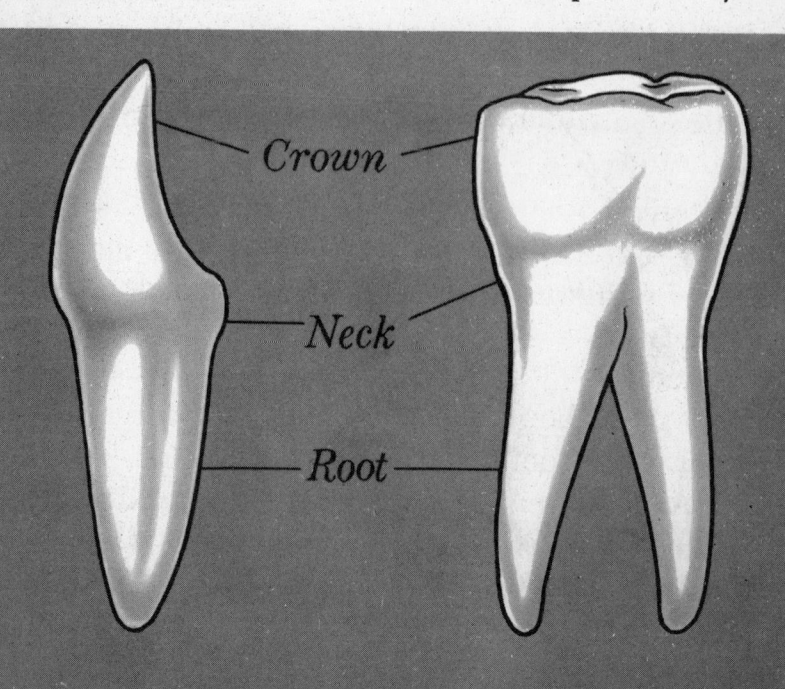

PARTS OF TWO KINDS OF TEETH

Enamel
Dentine
Pulp chamber
Gum

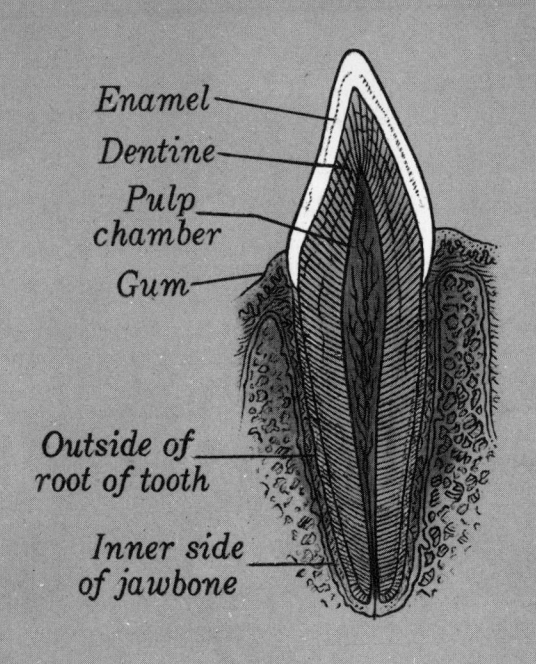

Outside of root of tooth
Inner side of jawbone

LOOKING INSIDE A TOOTH

make the best use of these foods. All the good health rules are good tooth rules."

Jean thanked the dentist for telling her so much about teeth and their care.

"Jean is a very good patient,*" the dentist said to her mother. "Bring her here again in six months. Then I shall find any small cavities that should be filled. Don't wait to come until she has another toothache."

SIX MONTHS LATER

When Jean went to the dentist's six months later, he found only one very small cavity. He filled it quickly. Filling the tooth did not hurt Jean at all, because the cavity had been discovered before it had gone deep into the dentine and near the nerve.

The dentist told her that irregular,* or crooked, teeth may be caused in many ways:

1. By not having enough tough food to chew. Chewing helps to make the jaws wider and so makes room for the second teeth.

2. By adenoids. Adenoids often cause a child to breathe through the mouth. Breathing through the mouth may cause narrow jaws and crowding of the teeth.

3. By letting the first teeth remain in the mouth too long or by pulling them out too soon. The first teeth should help guide the second teeth in place.

Look at the picture below. In one jaw the teeth are crooked and irregular. In the other jaw they are straight. The dentist must begin early to straighten crooked teeth.

Other Children's Questions

These are questions that children have asked about teeth. Find the right answers to tell in class.

1. Which good health rules are good tooth rules?
2. What makes a tooth ache?

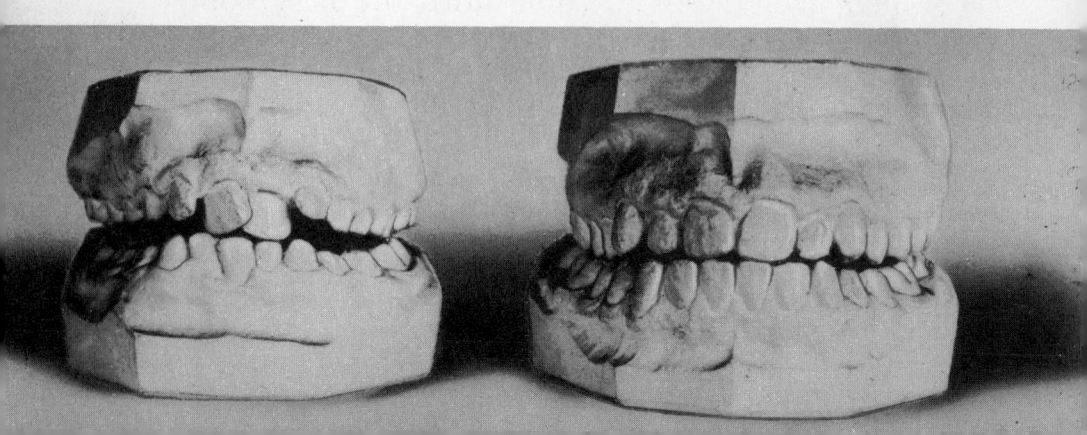

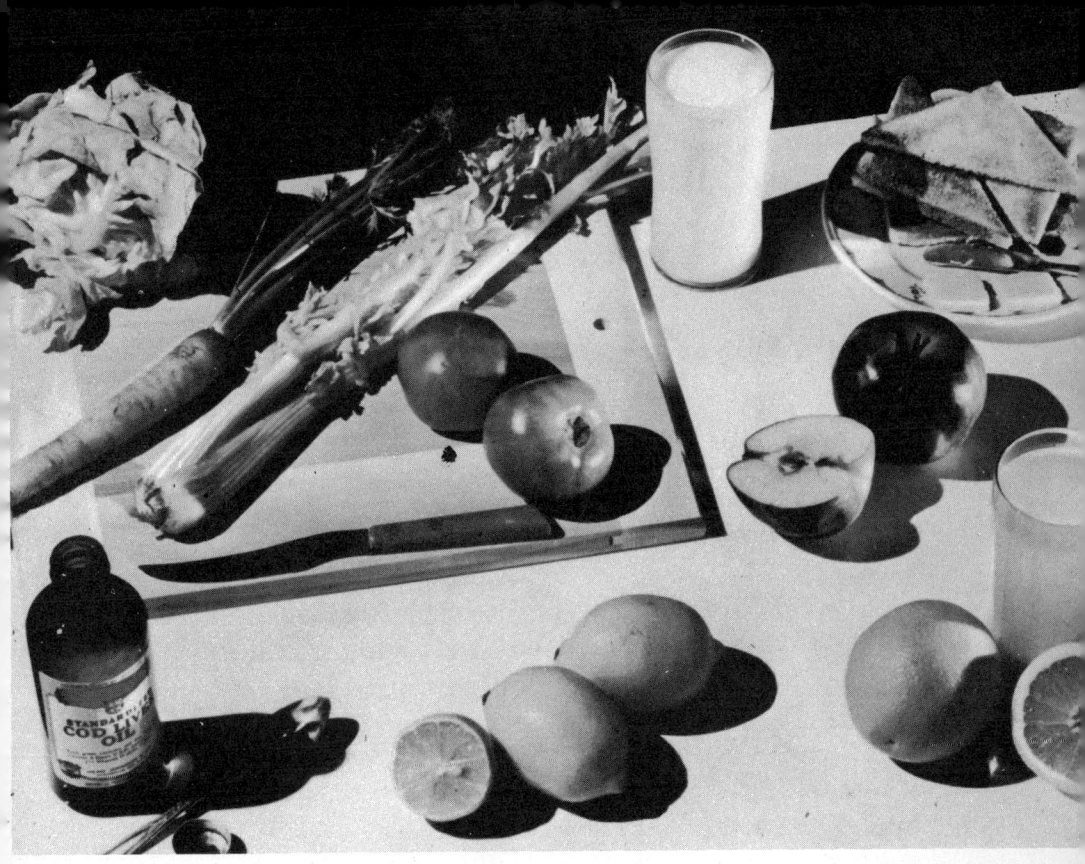

Find the Right Word

Here are seven sentences in which words are missing. Find the right word for each sentence. The words are: milk, teeth, chewing, cleaning, once, twice, small. (Do not write in this book.)

1. It is wise to have a dental examination —— a year.
2. Every day we should eat some foods that need much ——.
3. —— the teeth in the right way is important.
4. To help make strong teeth, we should have vegetables, fruit, and ——.
5. A hole in a tooth should be filled when it is ——.
6. Adenoids sometimes cause irregular ——.
7. When you have a toothache, you should go to the dentist at ——.

Things to Think About

1. How is an early visit to the dentist like a "stitch in time"?

2. How does one get a third set of teeth? Do you want to have a third set?

Things to Do

1. Collect from old newspapers and magazines everything you can find about teeth, tooth pastes, and toothbrushes. Put the best pictures and paragraphs on the class bulletin board or in the class scrapbook.

2. A boy or girl ten to twelve years old should have twelve teeth in his upper jaw. How many have you? Find the sixth tooth from the front. This is the first molar.* Make a chart for your health notebook showing the teeth in your mouth.

3. Have you been to the dentist within six months? Why should you not wait to go to the dentist until a tooth begins to ache? Talk over these questions with your mother. Tell the teacher what she said.

4. Brush your teeth carefully at least twice a day. Brush down over the upper teeth and up over the lower teeth. Be sure that every tooth is brushed. If your teeth are so close together that brushing does not clean out the bits of food caught between the teeth, use dental floss or dental tape. Brush over the gums, too, to help to make them firm and healthy. A mouthwash cannot do the work of a good toothbrush. A toothbrush should be small enough to fit into the mouth easily, and it should have stiff bristles that are rather far apart.

5. Make an exhibit of foods good for the teeth. Be sure to include milk, oranges, lettuce, celery, and cod-liver or other fish-liver oil. Make this exhibit for a parents' meeting or to put in a store or in the main hall of your school.

6. Draw a picture of a tooth and name each part.

PREVENTING DISEASE

DISEASES WE NEED NOT HAVE

There are five serious diseases that no one need have today. In the past these diseases killed many men, women, and children. Do you know which diseases they are? Do you know why no one need have them today?

The five diseases are smallpox,* diphtheria,* typhoid * fever, whooping * cough, and tetanus,* or lockjaw.

Smallpox can be prevented by vaccination.* A successful vaccination protects a person from smallpox for five to seven years. Vaccination is simple and safe to have done. Even a baby does not mind being vaccinated.* One baby just looked surprised when the doctor pricked his arm with the needle. It was over so quickly the baby did not even cry. Every child should be vaccinated at least every seven years, beginning with his first year. He should be vaccinated again whenever he knows he has been close to smallpox germs. Vaccination leaves only a little scar on your arm or leg. Do you wear this badge of protection?

Some persons are afraid vaccination will make them sick. They need not worry if they follow the doctor's directions. They should be sure to keep dirt and flies away from the vaccinated spot. The arm or leg may swell a little and feel sore. There may be a little fever and a headache. But the soreness, headache, and fever soon pass away and the person is then almost sure not to get smallpox.

Diphtheria is another disease that can be prevented in about the same way as smallpox. Diphtheria is most dangerous to young children. It causes the death of more young children than grownups. Two thirds of the people who die from diphtheria in cities are children under five years of age. For that reason every mother should have the doctor protect her baby from diphtheria when he is between six and nine months old.

Have you ever had the Schick * test? That is a test to find out whether or not you will get diphtheria if diphtheria bacteria get into your body. Being protected from bacteria that cause a disease is called *having immunity* * to the disease. If the Schick test shows that you do not have immunity against diphtheria, you should be protected with toxoid,* just as the little baby is.

Other ways of preventing diphtheria are to kill the bacteria on all articles used by a person who has diphtheria and to make milk safe by boiling or pasteurizing * it.

Typhoid fever is a third disease that no one need have. Typhoid vaccine * will prevent typhoid fever for a year or two. People should get this protection if there is danger of typhoid fever where they live. Many people have the typhoid vaccine given them before they go on trips to places where the water may not be safe. Even on short trips the water people get is often not so safe as the water they have at home. They must either kill the bacteria in the water by boiling it or by treating it with a substance called chlorine.* If they do not do this, they should gain immunity against typhoid fever before they start on the trip.

The fourth disease, whooping cough, should become much less common. For many years a whooping cough vaccine was used, but whooping cough did not disappear. Now a better vaccine has been made from certain kinds of whooping cough bacteria. With this new vaccine the results are very much better. It does not protect everyone, but it will protect about seven out of ten who take it.

The fifth disease that we need not have is tetanus, or lockjaw. This disease is most often caused by certain bacteria getting into a wound. Every U.S. soldier, sailor, and marine in World War II was given tetanus toxoid. As a result there were only a few cases of tetanus. Most doctors think every child should be protected with tetanus toxoid.

Here is a good plan for getting immunity:
>   At six months of age, whooping cough vaccine
>   At nine months of age, diphtheria toxoid
>   At one year of age, tetanus toxoid and smallpox vaccination
>   Typhoid vaccine whenever there is danger of typhoid

Anyone can have tuberculosis,* too, but it need not be you. The doctor can give you a test to see if tuberculosis germs are in your body. This is a simple test. It does not hurt. If the test says *Yes,* the doctor will want to take an X-ray picture of your lungs. Then he will tell you what to do.

TWO DISEASES THAT ARE HARDER TO PREVENT

Measles and scarlet fever are harder to prevent. Some day we may be able to get immunity from these diseases as surely as we now get immunity from smallpox, diphtheria, and typhoid fever. The best thing we can do now is to prevent the spread of measles and scarlet fever.

Measles is caught easily. When it begins, it is like a cold. Then others are likely to catch it. This is another reason why boys and girls with new colds should stay home and away from babies and other children for two or three days. Perhaps the new cold is the beginning of measles.

Scarlet fever is another dangerous disease. It may cause deafness, a weak heart, or other injury.* Any person who has scarlet fever should be kept away from everybody except his doctor and the person who is taking care of him. You should never go into a house that has a scarlet fever sign on it. Keep far away from the bacteria that cause scarlet fever.

Scarlet fever bacteria cause sore throat and a rash * in one person. The same bacteria may cause only a sore throat and no rash in another person. Sore throats caused by these bacteria are just as dangerous as cases with the scarlet fever rash.

WHY HELEN'S CLASS DID NOT CATCH SCARLET FEVER

One morning Miss Black, Helen's teacher, noticed how pale Helen looked. Helen usually had red cheeks.

"Do you feel as well as usual, Helen?" she asked.

"No, my throat is sore," Helen told her, "and my head feels hot."

"You should go to see the nurse right away,

Helen. You know where her office is. If she is not there, stay in the little room next to her main office. Stay there by yourself and wait for her. Do not go near any other children."

Helen did just as Miss Black said. When the nurse came, she looked at Helen's throat and took her temperature. Then the nurse telephoned Helen's mother.

"Hello, is this Mrs. Brown?" the nurse said. "This is the school nurse. I have just taken Helen's temperature and it is high. She has a fever. It may be scarlet fever. Can you come for her right away?"

While Helen was waiting for her mother, she sat in the little room all by herself. The nurse told Helen how important it was to keep other people from catching any disease she might have. These are the three things she told Helen she must always do:

1. Stay at home if you are beginning to catch cold.

2. Come to the nurse's office if you begin to feel ill in school.

3. Stay away from other children until you find out that you do not have a disease that is catching.

Helen remembered these three rules. She was very ill, but no one caught scarlet fever from her.

HOW BOYS AND GIRLS CAN HELP

The school doctor and nurse try to keep diseases out of school. But they cannot do this unless all the boys and girls help. They can help in these ways:

1. They can go to the doctor or nurse if they begin to get a sore throat, running nose, headache, or rash on the skin during the school day.

2. They can go to the doctor or nurse if their eyes are red and sore.

3. They can go to the school doctor or nurse before they enter the classroom the first day they return to school after an illness.

4. They can obey all the doctor's and nurse's orders.

Other Children's Questions

Answer as many of these questions as you can. You will find the answers to some of them in the pages you have just read. The best way to get the answers to the others is to ask a doctor or nurse.

1. Does vaccination make you sick?
2. Why is it necessary to be vaccinated?
3. Would I get chicken pox if I went to see a child who had chicken pox?
4. Why does a doctor take a person's temperature?
5. Why did I have to stay home so long when I had whooping cough?

Things to Think About

1. Why should people no longer be afraid of smallpox, or diphtheria, or typhoid fever, or whooping cough, or tetanus?

2. If no one need have diphtheria, smallpox, or typhoid fever, why do thousands of children still die from diphtheria? Why did 14,000 persons in the United States have smallpox in one year? And why do 44,000 people in the United States and Canada have typhoid fever every year?

Matching

Match each of the "why" questions with the right "because" answer. (Do not write in this book.)

WHY?	BECAUSE
1. Why need no one have smallpox today?	Because they have been protected with toxoid when they were babies.
2. Why do fewer and fewer children have diphtheria now?	Because the water where they are going may not be safe to drink.
3. Why were all the soldiers in World War II given tetanus toxoid?	Because they might have serious wounds.
4. Why should persons who travel be given typhoid vaccine before they go away?	Because it can be prevented by vaccination.

Things to Do

1. Make posters that tell people they should
    (1) be vaccinated against smallpox.
    (2) have the toxoid treatment given to babies and children to prevent diphtheria.
    (3) have typhoid vaccine if they are living where the food and water are not clean.
2. Read this unit to your parents.
3. Make a scrapbook of interesting pictures for some child who has a catching disease. You cannot go to see him, but the scrapbook will let him know that you are thinking about him.
4. Find out the rules in your school that tell you how long you should stay out of school if you have measles, mumps, scarlet fever, whooping cough, or some other disease that is catching. Find out what you should do first when you come back to school after an illness.

Unit VI
ON PARADE

You are "on parade" every day. People are watching you. The way you sit and stand and walk tells them something about the kind of boy or girl you are. What does your posture say about you?

This unit tells why posture is important and what you can do to improve your posture.

This unit is also about good feet. Do you have an Indian walk? Do you know how to buy the right kind of shoes and stockings? This unit will tell you.

Good posture and good feet are only part of keeping fit. If you were to begin training on a baseball team, you would have to obey many rules. Read the last part of this unit to find out what some of these training rules are.

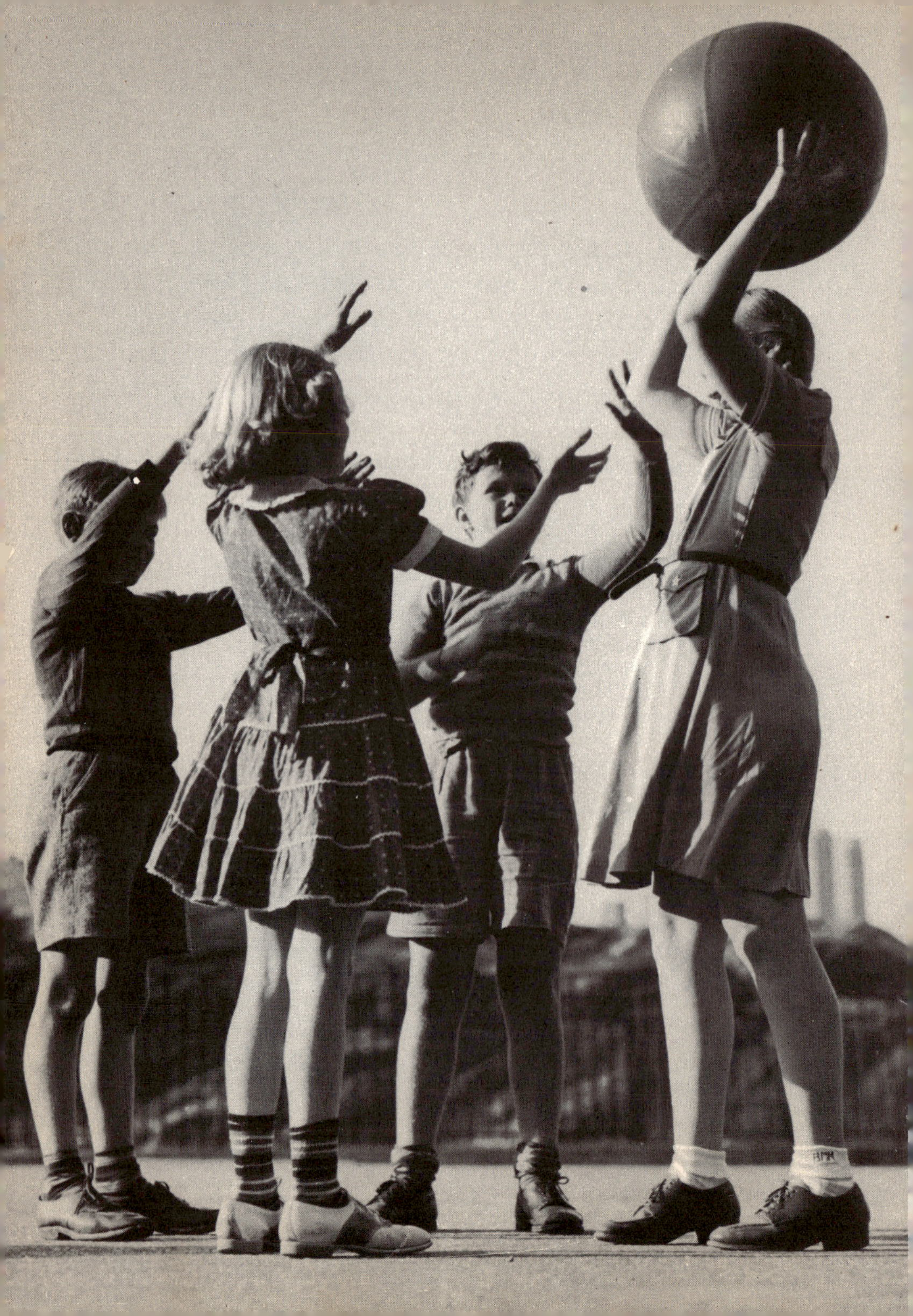

GOOD POSTURE IN SITTING AND STANDING

We spend much time during the day sitting or standing. Some boys and girls have the habit of sitting and standing in good posture. Others are learning to sit and stand better. Some still have poor posture. The first story tells how Jane's mother taught her to stand and sit like the pictures she was looking at.

JANE IN THE LOOKING GLASS

"I wish I looked like the people in these pictures," Jane said as she turned the pages of her book. The book was full of pictures of people standing or walking or sitting in good positions. Jane liked the people in these pictures.

"What can I do to look like the people in these pictures?" Jane asked her mother.

"Begin sitting in good posture now," her mother said. Jane suddenly threw back her shoulders and sat up stiff and straight.

"No, not like that!" her mother said. "The people in the pictures are not stiff and uncomfortable, as you are now.

"Sit down with your side to the long mirror. Now rest both feet on the floor, with both your heels and toes touching the floor. Don't bother about your shoulders. Your shoulders will take care of themselves."

WHICH ARE THE GOOD POSTURES?

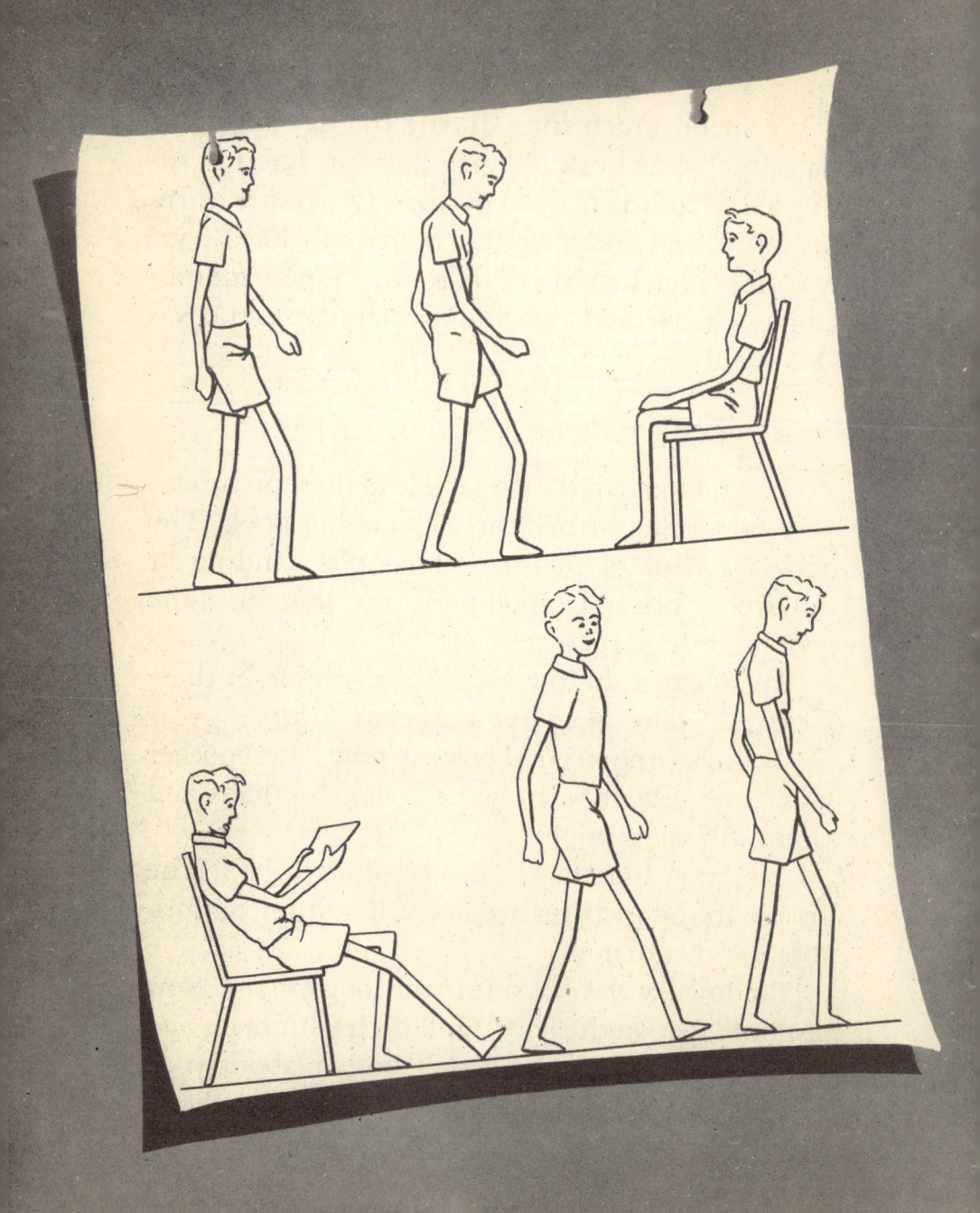

Jane found that her chair was just the right size. She could touch the floor easily. "Good posture is like a game," she said. "What do I do now?"

"Next you must pull in the muscles of your abdomen. Your abdomen becomes flat, up goes your head, and in goes your chin. Now look at yourself in the mirror and try to imagine that someone is lifting you up by a cord fastened to the top of your head. You are being lifted up—up—up, as tall as you can go. See how tall you are sitting—and how well. Do you feel comfortable, too?"

"Yes, I feel comfortable and—as though I were somebody important," said Jane.

"I know what you mean. It is a good feeling. Would you like to practice standing?"

"Yes," said Jane. "Tell me what to do."

"Point your feet straight ahead. That is fine! Now pull in your abdomen, as you did before, so that your head goes up high. Try to make yourself as tall as you can by stretching from the abdomen all the way to the top of your head. Don't make your knees stiff. Now you are standing tall and straight and at ease."

And Jane was, indeed. She looked very much like one of the pictures she had liked.

WHY GOOD POSTURE IS IMPORTANT

Good posture is comfortable. It causes no strain on any part of the body. One does not get nearly so tired standing or walking if his posture is good.

Lungs

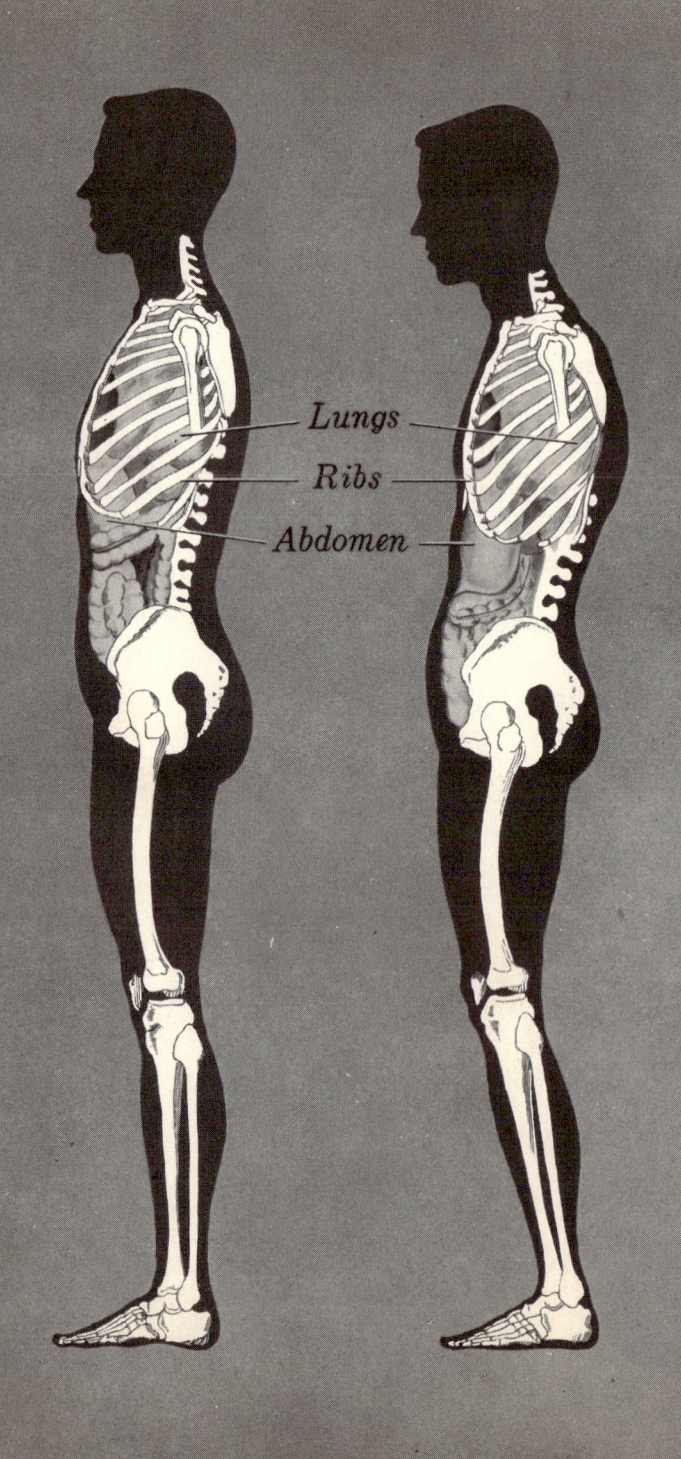

Ribs

Abdomen

Good posture gives the organs of the body all the room they need. One picture on page 116 shows a boy who is standing well and the other a boy who is standing poorly. In which do all the organs sag downward? When you are doubled over in a cramped position, it is harder to breathe deeply. The lungs cannot fill with air so easily, less oxygen is carried to the muscles, and the muscles of course do not work so well. It is also harder for the heart to pump blood to all parts of the body. Poor posture even makes the digestion * of food and regular bowel movements harder. So, you see, one of the things needed for good health is good posture.

Good posture is beautiful. It is a pleasure to look at persons who sit and stand well and who are at ease in action. Good posture helps one to be more popular. It also helps one to be a leader and to get a job.

When you sit, stand, and walk well, you feel more sure of yourself. This helps to make you happy.

To get and keep good posture, we must have good muscles. Good muscles are strong muscles that obey us quickly. Good muscles come with good health. Good posture, good muscles, good health come with all the good health habits you have learned.

BONES PLAY A PART, TOO

The bones also help us to have good posture. Run your hand down the center of your back. Do you feel the bumps all the way down? Those bumps are the bones of the backbone, or spinal * column. Good posture keeps all the bones of the spinal column in the right positions. That makes it easy for the muscles to keep the body upright. Sitting on one foot, slumping down in the seat, standing on one foot, or always carrying loads of books on the same side of the body throws the body into wrong positions. These wrong positions make some muscles do more than their share of work. The result is a feeling of strain and fatigue.

OTHER HELPS TO GOOD POSTURE

If your chair is too high, you cannot sit with both your heels and toes touching the floor. Your feet may even dangle. Jane said that her chair in school was too high.

"You should ask your teacher to have your seat and desk made the right height for you so that you can sit comfortably with your feet on the floor and your elbows at the level of the desk like this," said Jane's mother, as she drew the picture at the top of page 119.

"Give me the picture, Mother," said Jane. "I'll take it to school and ask Miss Stone if I may have my chair and desk made the right height. If the chair cannot be made the right height, I'll get a little footstool or else change to a seat and a desk that just fit me."

"That is a good plan," said her mother. "If your feet rest on the floor, you are more comfortable. The chair does not press on the blood vessels in the leg, and the blood can circulate more easily through the blood vessels."

Jane's brother, Bob, came in just in time to hear what his mother had just said. "My teacher says that poor eyesight may prevent good posture," he said.

"I can understand how it would," said Jane. "If you can't see well, you have to bend over close to the book or the paper at which you are looking."

"I think that feeling happy also makes a great difference in the way you sit and stand," their mother told them. "Watch people the next few days and tell me if you think I am right about this."

Bob picked up his books and started off to study them.

"Wait a minute," said his mother. She walked with him to the long mirror. "What is wrong here?" she asked.

Bob looked in the mirror and saw that the books were pulling him over a little to one side. "I should not carry the books in the same hand all the time, as I have been carrying them," he said. "I'll carry them first on one side and then on the other."

"That will help you to have good posture," said his mother.

OTHER CHILDREN'S QUESTIONS

What are the right answers to these questions, which other children have asked about posture?

1. Why should we sit straight?
2. What is the correct way to stand?
3. Does a cramped position make it harder to breathe?
4. Why should both feet rest on the floor when we are sitting?

FIND THE RIGHT WORD

The words which will complete the following sentences are: spinal column, touch, breathe, happy, beautiful, comfortable, tired out. Find the right words for the blanks. (Do not write in this book.)

1. Good posture is both ―― and ――
2. Poor posture makes it harder to ―― deeply.
3. Exercising until you are ―― will not build strong muscles.
4. Good posture keeps all the bones in the ―― in the right positions.
5. In sitting, heels and toes should ―― the floor.
6. Feeling ―― makes a difference in the way you sit and stand and walk.

THINGS TO THINK ABOUT

1. Why do happiness and good posture go together?
2. How may sitting bent over with the feet dangling keep the blood from circulating in the right way?

THINGS TO DO

1. If you have poor posture, learn how to correct the defects in the way you sit and stand and walk. Defects that

are not quickly corrected often grow worse, until the habit of poor posture is formed. Ask your teacher or doctor to tell you exactly what to do to make your posture better. Have your picture taken before and after.

2. Is your chair at home so high that your feet do not touch the floor? If it is, build yourself a footstool. Prepare three boards and nail them together. Ask your father or someone else to help you if you need help. Make the footstool high enough so that your feet rest on it easily when there is a square corner at your knees.

3. Look through magazines and books to find pictures of people who are standing, sitting, or walking in good form. Use these pictures to make a Good Posture Book or posters or paste them in your health notebook.

4. At recess some day have parades around the yard. First have a parade of children carrying books on their heads. Then imagine that you are all princes or princesses wearing crowns. Then have a parade of Indian chiefs.

5. Ask your mother to read to you the directions for standing and sitting which were given to Jane by her mother. While your mother is reading, follow each direction and see how well you look when you sit and stand according to these directions. Try to sit and stand in good positions every day until you have formed the habits of good posture.

FEET ON PARADE

The way we use our feet is almost as important as the way we use our heads. Tired feet make a tired person. Tired feet have spoiled many good times at parties or on trips. It is too bad to make a good pair of feet hurt by wearing the wrong kind of shoes and stockings.

FEET ON THE BEACH

When Jack was at the beach one day, he noticed people's feet as they walked by. Some of the feet were straight and brown. Some were crookèd and red in spots. Some seemed quite out of shape.

"Why are some people's feet so ugly?" Jack asked his mother.

"The wrong kinds of shoes are most to blame," she told him. "Some shoes are not shaped very much like feet. Many shoes, for example, have pointed toes. Are your feet pointed?"

Jack looked at his feet. "No," he said, "they are nearly straight across at the toes."

"And what do you think would happen if your toes had to go into pointed shoes?"

"I should think the big toe would be pushed back and sidewise," said Jack.

"Yes," said his mother. "A pointed shoe pushes against the big toe. The toe cannot go straight back; so it is bent outward at the joint. That makes the bumps, or enlarged joints, which you saw on some people's feet. Bunions * sometimes grow when these enlarged joints become very sore and painful."

"Bunions? I thought they were called corns," * said Jack.

"People have corns, too, and they come from wearing the wrong kinds of shoes. A shoe that is too tight crowds the toes. A shoe that is too loose rubs against the skin. Both kinds may cause corns."

"I know what they look like. They're hard spots on your toes, and they often hurt. Grandma says her corn feels like a little stone pressed down into her toe," Jack said.

"Did she tell you about the tight shoes she wore when she was a girl? She has always been sorry that she wore them. But shoes are not the only things that cause foot trouble. Do you know that stockings that are too short may hurt the feet, too?"

"No," said Jack. "I didn't think that stockings could hurt your feet. Stockings seem so soft."

"But when stockings are too short, they keep pulling the toes back and crowding them together, just as pointed shoes do," said his mother. "That is why you should buy both shoes and stockings that are a half inch longer than your feet."

THE INDIAN WALK

"Indians had good, strong feet, didn't they?" asked Jack.

"Yes, they did," said his mother. "They walked barefooted a great deal, or they wore soft, loose shoes called moccasins.

"Take a few steps along the beach, Jack, and let me see whether you have an Indian walk."

Jack had never heard of an Indian walk. He walked a little way on the beach and ran back.

"Now, Mother, do I have an Indian walk?"

His mother looked at his footprints. They looked like the picture on page 124.

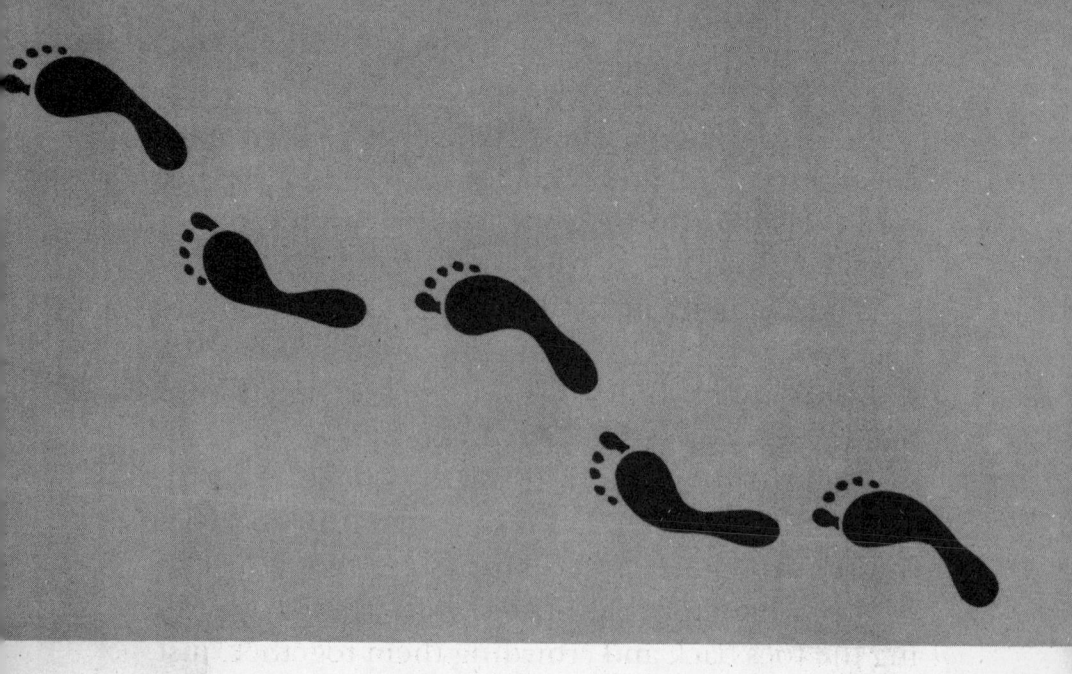

Each footprint pointed straight ahead—neither in nor out.

"Yes, you have an Indian walk," said Jack's mother. "Each foot points straight ahead."

"Here is someone who does not have an Indian walk," said Jack, looking at another footprint in the sand. "See how the toes point out!"

A GOOD ARCH *

"Take a step on this soft, wet sand, and we'll see whether or not you have a good arch," Jack's mother told him.

"What is an arch?" said Jack.

"Think a moment. What is the arch of a bridge?" his mother asked him.

"The arch is the curved part that holds up the bridge," Jack said.

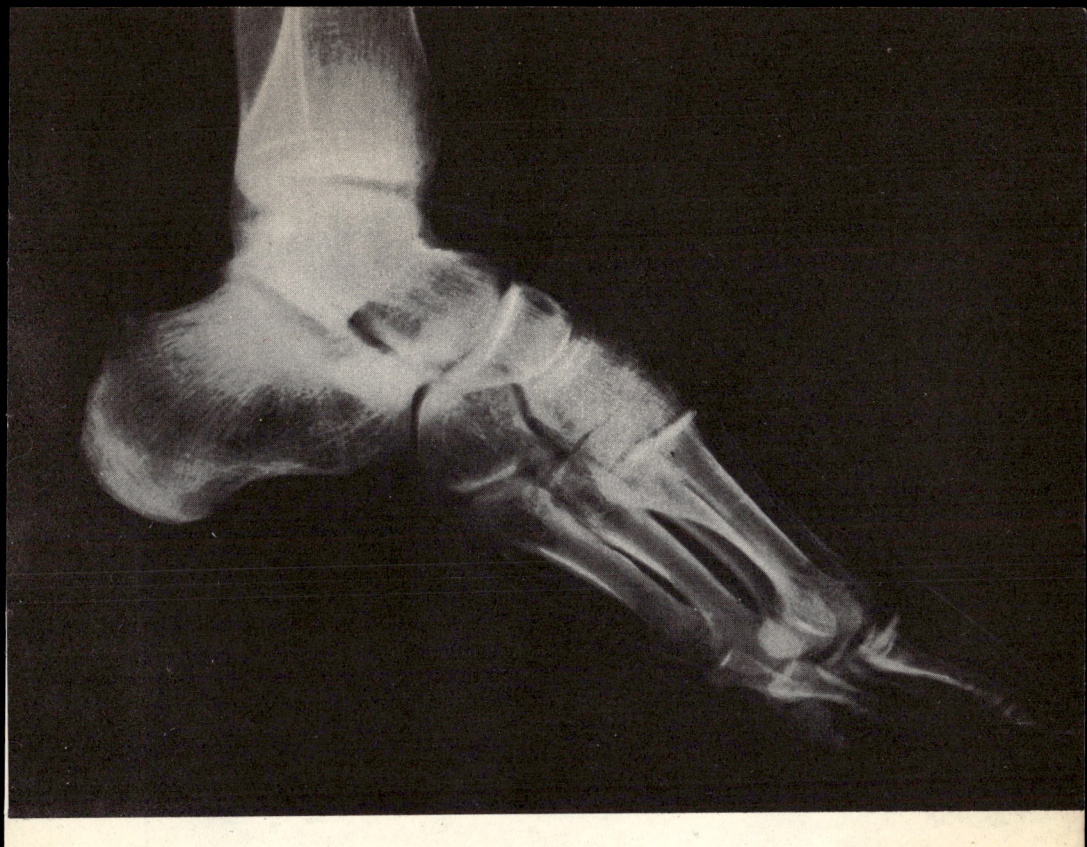

"The arch of a foot is a curved part that holds up the foot," his mother explained. "There are many small bones in the foot. Some of these form the lengthwise * arch. Put your hand under your foot and feel this arch. The bones of course are covered with muscle and skin. A good arch has strong muscles which hold the bony arch up firmly.

"Now make your footprint on the sand, and we shall see what kind of arch you have—firm or flabby."

Jack took two steps and then looked at his footprints. They looked like those you see on page 124.

Jack was disappointed. "They are not good foot-

125

prints," he said. "Each one looks as if a bite had been taken out of one side. I'll try again."

The second prints were just like the first.

"You should be glad, Jack," said his mother. "Those prints show that you have good arches. People with good arches usually put most of their weight on the outer side rather than on the inner side of their feet. If your footprint did not have, as you said, a bite out of one side—if it were rounded out on each side like the prints below, it might show that you had a fallen arch, or what some people call flatfoot."

"Oh," said Jack, very much pleased, "then I have an Indian walk and a good arch. The footprints on the sand show it."

"You wear shoes that are right for you," said Jack's mother. "You walk as you should. There is something else you do to keep the arches of your feet strong and your feet comfortable and well shaped."

"What is that?" asked Jack.

"You keep the rules of health that you know. Good food, exercise, and rest do much to help keep feet strong. People who have been ill or who have let themselves become very tired day after day often suffer from pain in the feet and legs. Their arches have become weak. They must build up their health before they will be able to have strong arches again."

The health of every part of the body depends on the health of the whole body.

Which Is Right?

1. Good food, exercise, and rest help us to have strong arches.
   Good food, exercise, and rest have nothing to do with having strong arches.
2. Shoes and stockings should both be exactly the same length as the feet.
   Shoes and stockings should both be a half inch longer than the feet.
3. We should walk with our toes pointed out.
   We should walk with our toes pointed straight ahead.
4. We should put most of our weight on the outer side of our feet.
   We should put most of our weight on the inner side of our feet.

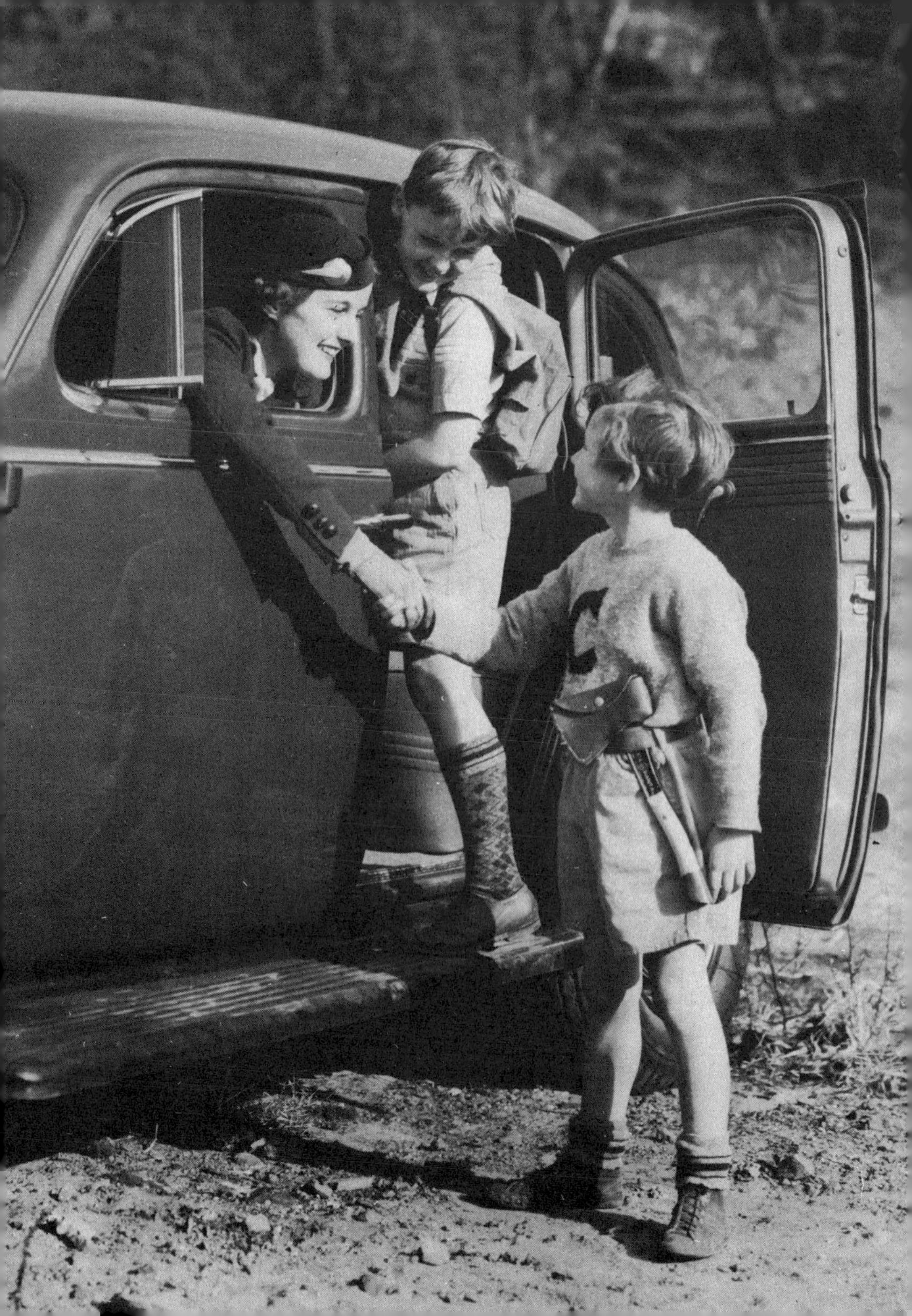

5. If you have a good arch, your footprint has a bite out of one side like the prints on page 124.
   If you have a good arch, your footprint is rounded out on each side like the prints on page 126.
6. We should wear shoes with pointed toes.
   We should wear shoes with rounded or square toes, like those that the children in the picture on page 128 are wearing.

Things to Think About

1. How can you prevent your feet from becoming ugly and sore?
2. Explain why some persons have fallen arches.

Things to Do

1. Do you have an Indian walk? Practice walking with your toes pointed straight ahead. Practice standing with your weight on the outer side of your feet.
2. Before you go with your mother to buy your next pair of stockings, measure your feet. Then buy stockings that are a half inch longer than your feet.
3. If you have a fallen arch or other foot defect, you can do exercises that will help correct it. These exercises are called corrective * exercises. The following are three corrective exercises that help to make the muscles of the feet stronger:
   (1) Pick up marbles or a pencil with your bare toes.
   (2) Scoop up sand with the outside edge of your feet.
   (3) Toe in; then teeter back from the toes to the heels and back again to the toes.
4. When you are washing your hands before going to bed, take time to wash your stockings, too. Some people wash their feet and their stockings every day. They always have clean feet in clean stockings.

5. If you have a blister * caused by your shoe rubbing on your foot, take proper care of it. Put a dot of iodine * on it. Prick the blister with a needle that has been held in a flame. Then put on a sterile * bandage,* held by adhesive * tape. If the blister is broken, wash the place with alcohol * and put a bandage on it.

IN TRAINING

Bill noticed that his big brother had stopped smoking. He asked him why.

"I've stopped smoking because I'm on the baseball team," he said. "The coach said, 'No smoking.'"

"What is a coach?" asked Bill.

"A coach is the man who trains the team. He shows the fellows how to catch and bat and throw the ball. He shows them how to work together and how to keep in the best of health. He helps the team to win the games."

"And why does he say, 'No smoking'?" asked Bill.

"He told us the reasons," said Bill's brother. "I'll tell you if you want to hear."

"Yes, I do," said Bill. "I hope to play on a team sometime."

"The first reason the coach gave was that smoking cuts down the 'wind.' You know what that means—you can't run so far or so fast without getting out of breath. You need to have good wind to make a home run. Smoking a pack of cigarettes a day may make a person more likely to puff when he runs.

"Second, smoking sometimes makes people restless and nervous.* And of course a good baseball player must not be nervous. Suppose that I am playing an important game. All the bases are full. I come up to bat and feel so nervous that I can't hit the ball. I'm not going to take the chance of letting cigarettes lose a game for our team.

"Third, smoking may hurt the heart. In fact, it's almost certain to hurt a weak heart. A heart that has been hurt by smoking or other causes is not a good heart for a baseball player to have.

"You will not find much smoking on a good team or among the fellows who get the highest marks in school. These boys either do not like to smoke or think that smoking keeps them from winning success in sports and in schoolwork.

"Some grownups say that smoking does not hurt them. Others have given up smoking because they found it was bad for them. Some people stop smoking because their throats feel better when they do not smoke. Some stop smoking because they would rather spend their money for something else. Still others stop smoking on doctors' orders.

"The coach said: 'No smoking and no drinking on the team while I am the coach.' Drinks with alcohol in them make a person less steady. Tests have shown this. Suppose that you have a pencil and try to put it into a little hole as many times a minute as possible. The steadier your hand is, the faster you can fit the pencil into the hole. You will make a high score. If you have taken even a small amount of an alcoholic * drink, your hand will be less steady. You will make a lower score. The coach wants steady players on his baseball team. So he says, 'No drinking.'

"There is one queer thing about alcohol. It makes people think they are making higher scores than usual, when they are making lower scores. It makes people think they are more steady than usual, when they are really less steady. It makes people think they are brighter than usual, when they are really duller. No one is the better for taking an alcoholic drink, while many persons are worse off for taking it."

Bill's father had come in while the boys were talking. "There's another danger we should keep in mind," he said. "Can you guess what danger I am thinking of?"

"Taking dangerous drugs * that no doctor has ordered for us," said Bill's brother.

"Yes," said his father. "There are laws against the sale of such drugs."

"What are these drugs?" asked Bill.

"The drugs I am speaking of are habit-forming * drugs. They make people want more and more of them. These drugs take away freedom. They make a person their slave. The person cannot get along without them. Once is far too often to take these drugs. Hundreds and hundreds of people have become slaves to drugs. They cannot break the habit. They say, 'We would give anything in the world to break the habit.' 'Touch not, taste not, handle not' —that's the rule if you ever are offered any alcoholic drink or any drug."

"One of the boys in school says, 'Touch not, taste not, the handle's hot!' " said Bill's brother.

His father laughed. "Good enough! The handle *is* hot. Remember the hot handle that drugs and alcohol have. People who touch and taste are likely to get badly hurt."

" 'No coffee or tea' is a training rule," said Bill's brother. "If a person drinks coffee or tea, he is likely to drink less milk. Milk is needed for growth and health. Coffee often makes a person so wide awake that he does not get enough sleep. Sleep is important. It is hard to be ready and quick during a whole game if one has not had enough sleep."

OTHER CHILDREN'S QUESTIONS

Children have asked the following questions. If you are sure you know the right answer, write it on a piece of paper. If you do not know the answer to a question, read these pages again to find the answer. Then write it.
1. Does tobacco hurt grown-up people?
2. Do the brightest boys in school smoke?
3. Why do some people stop smoking after they have begun?
4. Is "Do not drink tea or coffee" a training rule?

GOOD TRAINING RULES

You must keep the training rules if you want to be at your best. Complete the following rules. Read earlier pages again if you cannot fill in the blanks. The words to fill in the blanks are: wash, vegetables, colds, milk, part, eleven, smoking, alcohol. (Do not write in this book.)

1. I should drink —— three times a day.
2. Every day I should eat some fruit and ——.
3. I should play outdoors —— of the day, but I should not get overtired.
4. I will never form the habits of —— or taking drinks with —— in them.
5. I should sleep about —— hours a night.
6. I should always —— my hands and face before eating.
7. I should stay away from people who have —— and other diseases I might catch.

Things to Think About

1. Do football players have to be coaxed to eat a good breakfast? Why not?
2. Why is a member of a team a poor sport if he does not do everything he can to keep in good health?

Things to Do

1. Ask someone you know who is on a team what the training rules are. Make believe you are on a big team, too, and obey the same training rules.
2. Ask someone you know who has stopped smoking why he does not smoke any more.
3. What good health habits have you read about in these last pages? Add them to your list.
4. Stop reading a minute. How far from your eyes are you holding your book? Measure the distance with a ruler. Is it about fourteen inches?
5. Have you had milk instead of tea or coffee this week? If you cannot truly answer this question by saying, "Yes," this week, be sure you can say, "Yes," next week.

Unit VII

FOOD PROBLEMS

Boys and girls all over our country have learned to raise vegetables and fruit. Their families now have a better diet * than some families used to have. Other boys and girls have learned to raise chickens. Their families now can have eggs every day. Still other children have learned how to feed cows so that they will give more milk.

Grownups are working all the time to supply everyone with good, safe food all the year round. There are many problems in producing food, sending it to market, and selling it.

Read this unit to find out more about our daily foods: how to raise them, how to buy them, how to use them.

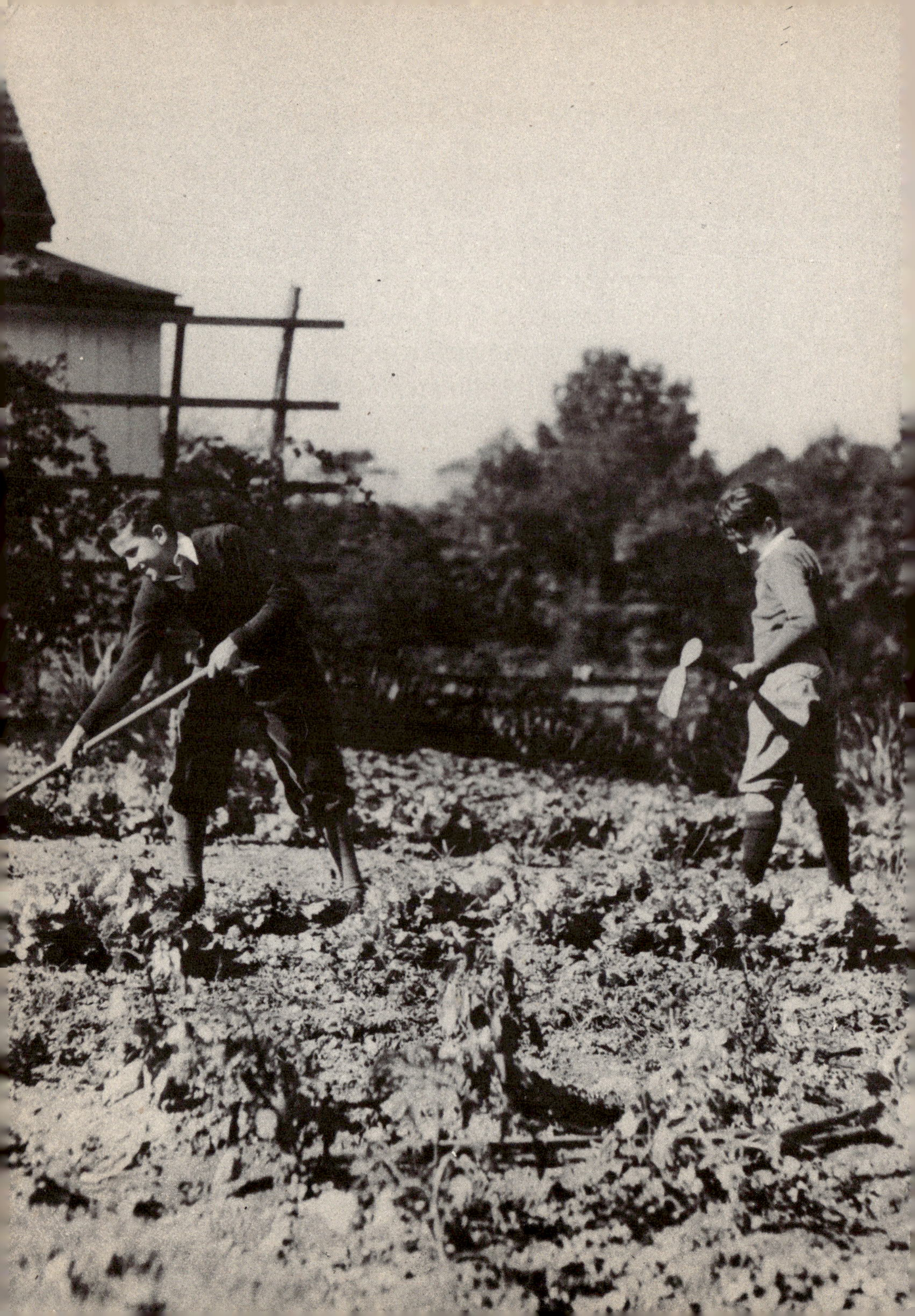

VEGETABLES

All vegetables are good for us. Some kinds we need every day. On our list of vegetables we should surely have green and yellow vegetables; tomatoes, fresh or canned; and some vegetable we can eat raw, that is, without cooking.

For breakfast we often have tomato juice. In a good dinner we find potatoes and a green-leaf vegetable. In a healthful supper we find carrots or another good vegetable.

How can we be sure to have plenty of fresh vegetables? Wouldn't it be fine to have your own vegetable market? That is what everyone with a vegetable garden of his own has. The next story tells what one boy did to supply his family with fresh vegetables.

A CITY BOY'S GARDEN

Fred and Tom were cousins. Fred lived in the country, and Tom lived many miles away near the city. One cold March day when Tom came home from school, he found a letter from Fred in the mailbox. This is what the letter said:

Dear Tom,

I have had a lot of fun tonight. You'd never guess what I've been doing, so I'll tell you. This morning the fellows at school were talking about starting our baseball team again. That means it's almost spring and it made me think of my garden. I plan to raise a lot of vegetables this summer.

Dad said that he was too busy with the apple trees to

have time for a garden this year and Mom was sorry. She thinks vegetables that are grown in your own garden are fresher and better than those you can buy at the store. I told her I'd plant a big garden for her this year. Tonight I've been going through seed catalogs planning what I want to grow. We need fresh vegetables all summer long and some that will keep for winter.

You should see the list I've made out. The pictures in the catalog look good enough to eat. I wish you were here to help me. We'd have fun. But I suppose you've never raised any vegetables. Maybe you can come here for a visit this summer and I'll show you how.

Well, Mom says it's eight o'clock and time for me to go to bed. Write and let me know if you can come this summer.

Your cousin,
Fred

That letter made Tom wish he lived in the country, too. He had always wanted to have a garden. He looked out the kitchen window. No, there wasn't room for much of a garden of any kind in the tiny back yard.

Suddenly he had a fine idea. There was an empty lot next to the house with a big "For Sale" sign on it. So far nobody had bought it. It had a high fence all around it and a gate that was locked. Maybe he could have a garden there.

That night after dinner Tom showed Fred's letter to his mother and father.

"Why can't I have a garden, too, Dad?" he asked. "There's plenty of room in that empty lot."

"Well, I don't know, Tom. We'd have to find out

first if it would be all right for you to use it. What do you think, Mother?"

"You know how much I like fresh vegetables," said Mrs. Norton. "I think Tom's idea is a good one—if it's all right for him to use the empty lot."

The next day Tom stopped at a seed store on his way home from school and got a seed catalog. He was almost sure that the owner of the empty lot would let him have his garden in it.

Sure enough, the first thing Tom's father said that evening was, "Well, Tom, I guess it's all right for you to begin on your garden any time. I saw Mr. Hill today. He was quite pleased about having a garden in his lot. It has good soil. It will make good use of the rain. It has a fence to keep out animals. You can make a fine garden there."

"Hurray," shouted Tom. "I knew he would let me have it. Let's decide tonight what we want to raise. I have a seed catalog. What do you want most, Mother?"

"In summer I like to have plenty of tomatoes," answered Mrs. Norton. "They are so red and juicy, and they taste so good when you pick them fresh from the vines. Some people say that tomatoes are hard to grow, but they're very good for us."

"I'll raise all you want," said Tom. "I'll buy plenty of tomato seeds."

"But you don't plant tomato seeds, Tom," Mr. Norton said. "You'll have to get small tomato plants and set them out to grow."

"Oh, I didn't know that. I'm learning already. What other vegetables shall I raise?"

"I'd like to have plenty of peas," said his mother. "Even the freshest peas you buy in the store do not taste quite so sweet as those you pick in your garden just before dinner. And I wish you would plant some rows of carrots and beets. Small, young carrots are delicious, and you cannot often buy beet greens in the store."

"Be sure to plant some Swiss chard," said Tom's father. "It's a fine green vegetable. You pull off the outside leaves, and new ones keep growing all summer."

"I'd like to plant some pumpkins for Halloween and for pumpkin pie," said Tom.

"When you look through the seed catalog, you will want to have all the vegetables there are. But you'd better just raise as many as you can take care of. Mother and I will pay you for your fresh vegetables," said his father.

That evening Tom wrote to his cousin Fred. He told him he was going to have a garden, too, and that he would not have time for a visit this coming summer.

Tom's father paid a man to put two inches of manure * on the ground and then plow it. After the ground was ready for planting, Tom did most of the work himself. He planted radishes, green onions, spinach, tomatoes, lettuce, Swiss chard, peas, carrots, beets, and pumpkins. During the spring and summer months he spent many hours hoeing his vegetables and pulling weeds. Often in the early evening before it got dark and on Saturday afternoon his father would work in the garden with him. "It's great to work out of doors after I've been in an office all day," he said.

Before long Tom pulled some radishes and green onions for lunch. Another day he brought in some small carrots which he had pulled out so that the others could grow bigger. How crisp and sweet they tasted when Tom and his father and mother ate them raw on a picnic!

The spinach grew very fast. Tom had planted that as a surprise. One day he filled his basket with the crisp green leaves and took them to his mother.

"How nice!" she exclaimed. "I didn't know you had planted spinach. Fresh spinach is sometimes hard to buy in the stores." She washed the leaves carefully and cooked it only a short time. They all said it was the best spinach they had ever tasted.

Perhaps the most exciting day was the one on which Tom brought in the first ripe tomato. It was a very large tomato, and it helped make a delicious lettuce and tomato salad for the family.

All summer long Tom kept bringing in fresh vegetables from the garden. Sometimes his mother would make a creamy vegetable soup. Sometimes she chopped raw carrots, cabbage, and apples together and made a very good salad. Sometimes she served carrots and peas together.

When frost came, the garden was bare of its bright vegetables and leaves. But in the cool part of the cellar were some big pumpkins, and on the window sill in the kitchen some green tomatoes were slowly ripening in the sun. Tom's mother used some of the pumpkin buttered as a vegetable for dinner. She used some for bowls of pumpkin and milk for supper. One pumpkin became a Halloween jack-o'-lantern, and one turned into the Thanksgiving pie.

"Raising vegetables was a fine idea, Tom," his father said. "Here is the money for them. You have earned it, and you may spend it as you wish."

"You have earned more than money could buy," said his mother. "We have better appetites and feel better this year than ever before—thanks to your garden, I believe."

"Having the garden was fun, too," said Tom. "Thank you for the money. Guess what I'm going to do with it."

There was enough money to buy the skates and skis Tom had been wishing for. Now he could spend his winter hours out of doors with the other boys and girls who went skating and skiing.

WHY VEGETABLES ARE GOOD FOR US

Tom's mother gave some reasons why she was glad to have vegetables from the garden. Do you remember what they were? She liked the taste of the fresh vegetables, and she thought they helped to keep the family well.

Vegetables reach down in the ground with their roots and get many minerals * that they find there. They store these minerals in the parts we eat. These minerals in our food help to keep us well.

One of the important minerals is iron.* Iron is needed for the blood. Without it the blood could not carry oxygen to the lungs. Without enough iron the body machine could not keep running smoothly.

All the vegetables Tom raised have iron in them: spinach, tomatoes, peas, beet greens, beets, Swiss chard, pumpkins, green onions, carrots, radishes, lettuce. Potatoes are important for their iron because we eat them every day. All these vegetables, you see, are real "iron mines."

EGGS ALL THE YEAR AROUND

Egg yolk also is rich in iron. That is one reason why most persons should have an egg a day. Although chickens lay more eggs in the spring than they do in the winter, we can have eggs all the year around. Eggs can be kept fresh in many ways. Sometimes they are frozen at a low temperature. Freezing eggs is a very good way to keep them fresh. Often they are kept in cold * storage until they are used. They may be put in a substance called *water* * *glass*.

Water glass keeps eggs fresh by keeping the air away from them.

Matching

Put the words in the left column with the right words in the other column. (Do not write in this book.)
1. Iron
2. Water glass
3. Oxygen

is a part of the air that is needed by all animals and plants.
is needed for the blood.
keeps eggs fresh.

Things to Think About

1. How do we know that vegetables, fruits, and milk help us to grow and keep well?
2. In what way is a garden like a mine?

Things to Do

1. Read this part of the unit to your father and mother when they have time to listen.
2. Plant some seeds, such as carrot seeds, in each of six small pots. Put the pots in a sunny window and give each pot enough water. When the plants have grown several inches, do these experiments with four of the pots:

(1) *Light*. Put one of your pots in a dark closet, but water it just as you water the other plants.

(2) *Warmth*. Put one of your pots out of doors for several days and nights.

(3) *Water*. Do not water one pot for several days.

(4) *Oxygen*. Set one pot in a pan of water and cover the pot and plants with a large glass jar. Now no more air can get to these plants.

What happens to the plants after a time?

Light is necessary for green plants. They cannot live forever in the dark. They cannot make food

145

unless they are in the light. They may grow in the dark as long as they can use food which they have already made. Plants may suffer from light that is too strong as well as from not enough light. Your carrot plants could not grow on the hot, dry desert.

A few plants in the cold arctic lands can grow at temperatures below 41°. Some germs and other very small plants can grow in water as hot at 176°. The best temperature for most plants and animals is between 68° and 86°. Is the temperature of your room about 68°? What is the outdoor temperature?

The leaves and stems and roots and seeds of plants are very largely water. A plant must have water in order to make food. The materials from which plants make food are taken out of the soil in water. Food is carried from one part of the plant to another in water. Water keeps the plant from being burned by the hot sun. Your garden is likely to be a success if it has enough water.

Plants must also have oxygen. There is plenty of oxygen in the air.

When plants are dried, it is found that half their weight is carbon.* They get their carbon from the carbon dioxide of the air. Although the amount of carbon dioxide in the air is very small, there always seems to be enough. Farmers do not have to worry about giving their plants enough carbon dioxide.

3. What kinds of vegetables do you raise in your garden? Tell the class how you help to care for them.

4. Ask one or two good farmers what vegetables they raise and how they store them for winter use. Ask them how they keep the soil from "wearing out."

5. Which vegetables are especially good to clean the teeth and help the blood to circulate in the teeth and gums? Look up *teeth* in the index. What else helps to make good teeth?

6. If you do not have a garden but have the ground on which to plant one, ask your father if you may help make a vegetable garden like Tom's. It will be worth the trouble to be able to have fresh vegetables every day. As soon as the ground is ready, plant vegetables for spring, summer, fall, and winter months.

7. Perhaps you can make an exhibit of good winter fruits and vegetables and good vegetables for summer, spring, and fall. If you cannot bring the vegetables and fruits to school, you can find pictures of them from seed books and magazines.

SAFE MILK

"Here comes the milkman," said Betty. "I'll bring in the bottles and clean them. Then I'll put them away in the coldest part of the icebox." She put the four quart bottles of milk next to the ice cubes. That was the coldest part of their electric refrigerator.

You already know that farmers try to have clean milk to sell. They keep the cows clean. They try to have the men who milk the cows clean and in good health. They put the milk in cans that have been washed and then scalded with boiling water. They keep the cans covered so that no dust or dirt can fly in.

The storekeeper does his part by keeping his milk clean, cold, and covered.

We should do our part in the home by keeping milk clean, covered, and cold.

Do you know why milk should be kept cold? No

matter how clean and careful the farmer is, a few harmful germs may be in the milk. These germs grow fast in a warm place in food that is good for them. Milk is a good food for germs as well as for people. If it is not kept cold, germs in it grow very fast. If they do, the milk is not fit to drink.

Germs may get into uncovered milk from the air or from people who are coughing or sneezing or talking near by. Germs may get into uncovered milk on the feet or wings of flies.

You can see that everyone who handles milk should always keep it clean, cold, and covered.

WHY SHOULD MILK BE PASTEURIZED?

If you look on the cover of your milk bottle, you will probably see the word *pasteurized*. Pasteurized milk has been heated to a temperature of 145°. It is kept at that temperature for a half hour. By that time almost all the harmful bacteria have been killed. The milk is then safe, even for a baby.

After it has been pasteurized, the milk is quickly cooled and sealed in cans or glass bottles. Or it is put in clean cardboard bottles. These cardboard bottles are used only once. Pasteurized milk is the safest milk to buy. If our milk has not been pasteurized, we can heat it ourselves at home. If we are in a hurry, we can bring the milk to the boiling point (212°). Then it will be safe to drink, but it will not taste so much like fresh milk as pasteurized milk does.

When we get a bottle of pasteurized milk that does not have two paper caps, we should wash off the top of the bottle. We can do this by holding it under water. It is better to wash off the germs on the rim of a glass bottle with water than to wash them into the milk as we pour it into a glass.

MINERALS AND VITAMINS

Milk is an important food because it contains minerals and vitamins. What do you already know about them? Here is a poem about minerals and vitamins.

> *Minerals* and *vitamins*
> Are words I heard today.
> They keep running through my head,
> No matter where I play.

Minerals I used to think
Were always found in stones.
But Mother said we must have some
Of them for teeth and bones.

Vitamins are things we need
Because they make us grow.
Just exactly what they are,
Some day I'm sure to know.

This I know, that minerals
And vitamins are found
In green and leafy vegetables
That grow above the ground,

In carrots, beets, and other things,
Each one a kind of root.
Vitamins are also found
In almost any fruit.

Milk is very rich in them.
It's rich in minerals, too.
I drink some milk at every meal—
One reason why I grew.

Find the Right Word

Here are some sentences in which words are missing. Find the right word for each blank. The words are: wash, safest, uncovered, covered, milk, vitamins, minerals. (Do not write in this book.)

1. Pasteurized milk is the —— milk to drink.
2. Milk should be kept clean, cold, and ——.
3. You should —— the top of a milk bottle that is not covered with a paper cap before you pour out the milk.
4. In milk there are —— and ——, which help us to have strong teeth and bones.
5. A good breakfast is as follows: orange juice, toast and butter, an egg, ——.
6. Germs grow very quickly in milk that is warm and ——.

Things to Think About

1. Why are some people, like the Eskimos, who drink little or no milk, able to grow and keep well?
2. Why has milk been called "the almost perfect food"?

Things to Do

1. Milk is used in making many things that we enjoy eating. Sour milk is used in some recipes, sweet milk in others. Get a cookbook and find twenty recipes in which milk is used. Copy the best one in your notebook.
2. Make a scrapbook of all the pictures you can find of milk and of butter, cheese, and other kinds of foods made from milk. Think of a good title for your book.
3. Make posters about the proper care of milk. A visit

to a dairy would help you to do this well. If you cannot go to a dairy, you can find pictures in books or magazines that will help you make the posters.

PLANNING MEALS

Mrs. Fealey had a large family and a small pocketbook. In her family were her husband, John; the five-year-old twins, Jerry and Judy; seven-year-old Nicky; nine-year-old John, Jr., and ten-year-old Peggy. In her pocketbook was just enough money to buy all the food for a day.

This morning Mrs. Fealey was busy washing clothes; so she let John and Peggy buy the food for a day. Miss White, the school nurse, had once told Peggy's class about the foods that should go into every family's market basket. Peggy now tried to remember just what the nurse had said.

John put the money in the very bottom of his pocket and stuffed his handkerchief down over it. Then he and Peggy started off for the store, carrying the market basket between them.

"The very first thing to buy is milk," Peggy said. "You add the number of quarts, John, while I say them. The twins should each have a quart of milk a day."

"That's two quarts," said John.

"Nicky should have a quart, and you and I should each have a quart," said Peggy.

"That makes five quarts," said John.

"Mother and Father are grownups. There should be a quart for them," said Peggy. "Each grownup should have a pint of milk a day, Miss White told us."

"That is six quarts all together," said John.

"Six quarts!" exclaimed Peggy. "That will cost a lot of money. But Miss White said we should get the milk first, no matter how much it cost."

So the first thing Peggy and John bought at the store was six quarts of milk. It came in paper bottles. The milk took about one third of their money.

"Bread and cereal come next," said Peggy. "Let's buy a box of oatmeal, two loaves of whole-wheat bread, and a day-old loaf of enriched* white bread. The day-old bread will cost only half price."

They spent about one tenth of their money for the bread and cereal.

John added the money spent for bread to the money spent for milk. "Say, Peggy," he said, "do you know we have not much more than half the money left?"

"I know," said Peggy. "And we still need some butter and fruit and vegetables."

"Here are some good, cheap apples," said John. "Let's buy five pounds of them."

"And here's a fine head of green cabbage. We can have some of it raw for lunch and the rest of it cooked for dinner."

"Father always wants potatoes for dinner. These old ones are almost as good as the new potatoes, and they are much cheaper. We'd better buy three pounds of them. I think, if we planned ahead and bought in larger quantities, we would save a little money on our food."

"Now let's see how much we have," said John.

    6 quarts of milk
    1 package of oatmeal
    2 loaves of whole-wheat bread
    1 loaf of white bread (day old)
    5 pounds of apples
    3 pounds of cabbage
    3 pounds of potatoes

They still had one fourth of their money.

"We ought to have a little butter," said Peggy.

"And this should be egg day. Have we enough money for a half dozen eggs?" said John.

BEFORE THEY WERE SENT TO MARKET THE EGGS WERE CAREFULLY PACKED IN BOXES.

"Eggs are cheap now," said the storekeeper.

"Then we'll take a half dozen," said John.

"Father would like a little bacon with his cabbage and potatoes. Let's spend the rest of the money on bacon, a can of tomatoes, and two onions," said Peggy. "Mother bought some brown sugar yesterday; so we don't need to buy sugar now."

This is the list of all they had bought:

    6 quarts of milk
    1 package of oatmeal
    3 loaves of bread
    5 pounds of apples
    3 pounds of cabbage
    3 pounds of potatoes
    ½ pound of tub butter
    ½ dozen eggs
    ½ pound of bacon
    1 can of tomatoes
    2 small onions

"We have just enough money!" exclaimed John, fishing the money out of his pocket.

When John and Peggy came home with the full market basket, their mother said, "Goodness, why did you get all that milk?"

"Miss White said that we should have a quart for every child under sixteen and a pint for every grownup. And it came to six quarts."

"Well, she ought to know," Mrs. Fealey said. "Now you may help me plan the meals."

The Fealey family had these three meals:

BREAKFAST

Oatmeal with raisins in it
Milk on the cereal and milk to drink
Toast and butter

LUNCH

Potato soup made with milk—a big bowl of it
Cabbage and apple salad
Bread and butter
Milk to drink

AFTER SCHOOL

A raw apple

DINNER

Baked potato
Eggs on toast
Stewed tomato and onion
Bacon
Green cabbage, cooked just enough to make it tender
Apple brown Betty made with apples, white bread crumbs, brown sugar, and cinnamon
Milk to drink

"This is a fine dinner," Mr. Fealey said that evening. "You'd better send John and Peggy marketing again, Mary."

Another day they had a one-dish dinner. Each had a big plate of beef-carrot-onion-potato stew. For dessert, they each chose a piece of fruit from a basket of fruit the children's uncle had brought them.

Build Better Meals

Good meals can be built from the seven main kinds of foods. Do you know what they are? If not, find them at the bottom of page 158. Add to each of the following meals a food that will make it a still more healthful meal. (Do not write in this book.)

BREAKFAST

1. Oatmeal
   Toast and butter
   Egg
   Milk

2. Orange juice
   Toast and butter

DINNER

3. Lamb chop
   Baked potato
   Bread and butter
   Milk

4. Spinach
   Mashed potato
   Rolls and butter
   Strawberries
   Milk

SUPPER OR LUNCH

5. Vegetable soup
   Whole-wheat bread
     and butter
   Fruit salad and cookies

6. Baked potato
   Bread and butter
   Baked apple
   Milk

Things to Think About

1. What is the cheapest breakfast you could have and still have a healthful breakfast?

2. What is the cheapest lunch you could bring to school and still have a healthful lunch?

Things to Do

1. Bring to school cut-out pictures of all kinds of things to eat. Lay them out on a long table, as food is spread out in a cafeteria. A cafeteria, you know, is a public eating place where you choose your own food as you walk along. Walk in line and pick up pictures of foods that would make you a good breakfast, lunch, or dinner.

2. Find out what the Pilgrims ate when they came to this country and what the Indians showed them how to raise.

3. Help your mother to plan your school lunch. Sometimes put up your own lunch.

4. Make a poster showing the amount of milk growing children should have each day. Make another poster showing the amount of milk that most grownups need.

5. Suppose that you had to do the marketing. What would you put in your market basket? What did John and Peggy put in first? Are the seven main kinds of foods in their list: (1) milk; (2) meat, fish, or eggs; (3) green and yellow vegetables; (4) oranges, tomatoes, grapefruit, or raw cabbage or other greens; (5) potatoes and other vegetables and fruits; (6) bread and cereals; (7) butter or other fat with vitamin A added?

Unit VIII

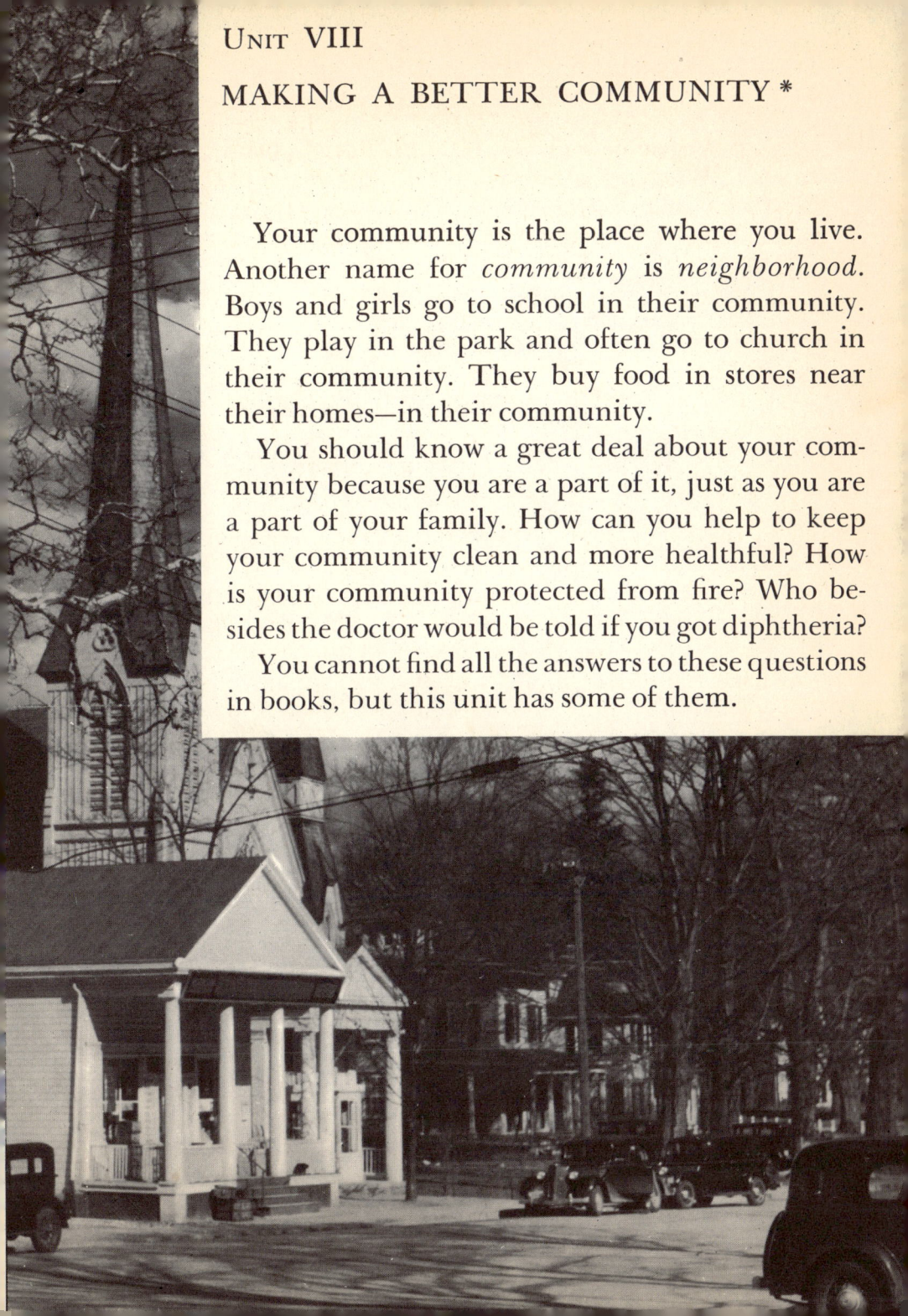

MAKING A BETTER COMMUNITY *

Your community is the place where you live. Another name for *community* is *neighborhood*. Boys and girls go to school in their community. They play in the park and often go to church in their community. They buy food in stores near their homes—in their community.

You should know a great deal about your community because you are a part of it, just as you are a part of your family. How can you help to keep your community clean and more healthful? How is your community protected from fire? Who besides the doctor would be told if you got diphtheria?

You cannot find all the answers to these questions in books, but this unit has some of them.

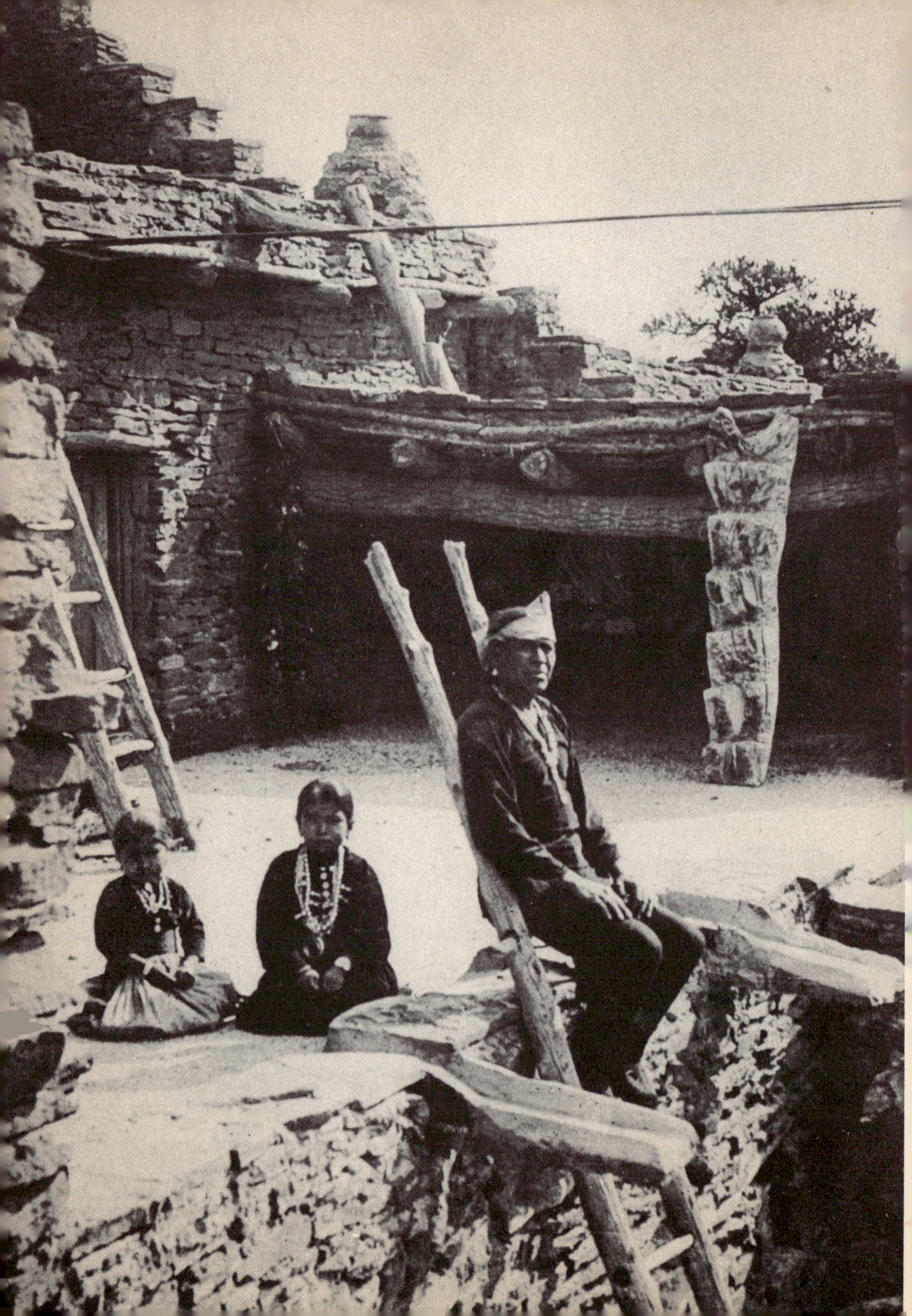

AN INDIAN PUEBLO

Before we read about our own communities, let us think first of a community that is quite different from ours.

A pueblo is an Indian town made of square mud houses that are usually painted white. The houses are two, sometimes three, stories high. They are built around a large, open space. In that open space the people of the town have their meetings, and the children play there.

The large, open space is kept very clean. There are never any toys or trash left about. The houses around the space are kept clean. Behind the houses are no piles of cans or garbage. The Indians living in the pueblos seem to know that one man's trash may mean another man's sickness. They take pride in the cleanliness and beauty of their pueblo.

HELPING YOUR COMMUNITY

Is your community as neat and clean as the pueblos of the Indians? Alleys behind the houses should be kept as neat as the streets in front of the houses. There should be no piles of trash or garbage anywhere near a town or city or near a house in the country.

Every person living in a town or city can do something nearly each day to help keep his own community clean, neat, and pleasing. Grown people raise grass and plant trees and flowers in their yards. They hire men to wash the streets, carry away trash and garbage, and take care of the parks. They pay other men to make sure that the drinking water is clean. Still other men do all they can to keep diseases from being spread. We call doctors and others who are paid to keep the community healthful health * officers.

Boys and girls, too, can do a great deal to help keep their community clean. They can begin by keeping their own yards neat. They can pick up orange peels, sticks, cans, broken bottles, and other trash and put them in the cans in which such things should go. Boys and girls can be careful never to leave any trash on streets, in parks, or in picnic places. A good citizen is always careful to keep his own house and yard clean, and he takes pride in helping to keep all public places clean. Being a good citizen means being a good member of your community.

Here are some stories of what boys and girls did in their community. Were they good citizens?

THE RAGWEED REGIMENT

One day in summer Donald's father said to some boys who had come to play with Donald, "How would you like to go to war tomorrow?"

The boys looked puzzled.

"I really mean it," said Donald's father. "The enemy is out in the vacant lots around here, 50,000 strong. This enemy uses pollen * to fight. It is like a kind of tear gas that floats in the air. Because of the pollen many people go around with running noses and red, watery eyes. As many as 70,000 people in one large city were attacked by this enemy."

"Do you mean the viruses that cause colds?" asked Jerry.

"It couldn't be viruses," said David. "They don't grow in vacant lots out in the sunshine."

Finally the boys said: "We give up. Tell us what the enemy is."

"Ragweed," said Donald's father. "It is one of four families of plants whose pollen gives hay fever to thousands of people. Billions and billions of grains of pollen float off in the air from late August until late September. They travel on the wings of the wind, sometimes for hundreds of miles. Come out with me and I will show you a ragweed plant."

The boys went with Donald's father to a vacant lot where ragweed was growing. The ragweed was about a foot high.

"This is just the right time to pull it out," said Donald's father. "If we wait until it has bloomed, it will be too late. We must pull it before there are any seeds, or we'll have the same work to do again next year."

The boys began with a will. They took hold of the weeds close to the ground and pulled. Because it has small roots, ragweed is easy to pull up. If dropped where it is pulled, it dries up in a day or two.

TWO KINDS OF RAGWEED

The boys called themselves the Ragweed Regiment. Every afternoon for a week they started out together and pulled up the ragweed in all the vacant lots near by. Soon there was not a single ragweed plant left standing to spread its pollen in late summer and to have seeds for next year.

The boys also learned these facts about hay fever:

1. Hay fever is not really a fever, and it is not caused by hay.

2. Hay fever is caused in 90 out of 100 cases by the pollen from plants. Ragweed and grasses cause most of the hay fever in the eastern part of our

country. Pigweed and Russian thistle and wormweed cause hay fever west of the Mississippi River. Around Denver, Colorado, about one third of the pollen in the air comes from sagebrush.

3. The doctor can prevent and cure hay fever by first finding out which kind of pollen is causing the trouble and then giving you what you need for immunity to pollen from that plant family. His treatment should cure hay fever sneezes and sniffles.

KILL A FLY IN MAY

"Buzz—buzz—buzz."

"Hello, what's this?" said Jean. "The first fly of spring."

"Buzz—buzz—buzz." It flew over to the dining-room table.

Jean took the wire fly swatter, which had not been used since last summer. She walked up to the table like a cat ready to jump on a mouse. She took a good aim. Swat! One dead fly.

Her grandmother said,
>"Kill a fly in May,
>And you'll keep thousands away."

"Is that true, Grandma?" asked Jean.

"Yes, in a way," said her grandmother. "The most important way to get rid of flies is to have no manure piles and other places where flies are hatched. All garbage cans should be kept covered. There should be no piles of garbage on any farm or in any town. Grownups should do most of the work of getting rid of flies. Children can help a little by killing flies in the spring.

"Not many flies live through the cold winter. This fly you killed could lay 120 eggs at a time three times during the summer. The first 120 eggs would hatch and we should have 120 flies. Each of these flies might lay 120 eggs and then, if all the flies lived, how many should we have?"

"One hundred twenty times 120; that would be 14,400 flies," said Jean, working it out on paper. "But of course not all of them would have lived. Now I'll keep my eyes open for the next fly that buzzes in. Why are flies dangerous, Grandma? They are so small. Most of them cannot bite."

"On their feet and wings flies carry bacteria that may cause disease. They drop these dangerous bacteria in milk, on other food, and on people's faces. That is why flies are so dangerous," Jean's grandmother told her.

That summer there were so many flies Jean couldn't sit on the porch without having them walk all over her. "I guess some people forgot to kill them in May," said Jean as she went indoors.

"Jean, Jean," called her grandmother, "do go back and shut the screen door. You left it open as you came in, and we'll have the house full of flies."

Jean went back quickly and shut the door she had left open.

"Will you please look at the window screens, too, to see if they are shut tight? There is no use in having screen doors and screens in the windows if they are not shut tight."

"During World War II," Jean's grandmother continued, "DDT* was used to get rid of flies and other insects. DDT or other sprays like it were used on the walls of barns and houses to cut down the number of flies. It did. But doctors later discovered DDT might make people ill. DDT must be used wisely. It may poison people. If carelessly used, it kills useful insects and birds."

Matching

Put the words in the left column with the right words in the other column. (Do not write in this book.)

1. DDT
2. Manure piles
3. Many bacteria
4. Screen doors
5. Ragweed

causes hay fever.
are places where flies are often hatched.
should be closed tightly.
may be used to kill insects.
are found on the feet and bodies of flies.

Things to Think About

1. Where do the flies that are in your community come from?
2. Which is better—
    (1) to kill all the flies you can or
    (2) to see that flies have no place where their eggs can be laid and hatched?
Give the reason for your answer.
3. Should you bother to pull up ragweed if you don't have hay fever yourself?

Things to Do

1. Tell your mother and father about ways of killing flies. Ask them how you can help get rid of flies in your neighborhood.

2. Buy a fly swatter and use it.

3. Follow a fly on one of its journeys and tell about all the places where it stops. Would you like to have that fly put its feet in your glass of milk or wipe them on your piece of bread and butter?

4. If you have screens in the windows, see that they are fastened tightly.

5. Find out whether or not you have plants growing in your community that cause hay fever. If you have, get some boys and girls to help you pull them up. Be sure to pull only harmful weeds.

COMMUNITY SPIRIT

Here are five very short stories about boys and girls who helped to make a better community. Have you or your friends helped to make a better community? What can you do now to help?

Jack hurried out the back gate to meet a friend and play ball. He noticed that his family's garbage can had been tipped over. The garbage had spilled into the alley. He picked up the garbage in some old papers and put it back in the can. He put the lid back on the garbage can.

Peggy and three of her friends ate a picnic lunch in the park. As soon as they were through eating, her friends wanted to go to another part of the park to play games.

Peggy said: "We must clean up all our trash first. Other people will want to picnic here."

They soon made the picnic spot as neat as they had found it.

Bob was going skating. As he left his house, he noticed that there was ice on the sidewalk where people passed. He went back to the house for a pail of ashes and scattered the ashes on the ice.

"Nobody wants to go skating here," he said to himself.

Mary and Margaret were walking in the park. The lilacs were in bloom. Margaret started to pick some flowers to take home.

"The lilacs in the park belong to everybody in

it," said Mary. "If nobody picks them, everybody can enjoy them."

"I didn't think of that," said Margaret. "It would not be fair for one person to pick them."

All one night the wind blew very hard. The next morning Bob saw that papers had been blown into his yard. He picked them up. Then he noticed that the vacant lot next door was full of dirty papers. Before he went to play ball, he spent five minutes picking up all the papers and putting them in a pile. He put a board on them so that the wind would not blow them away. When his father came home, he and his father had a bonfire.

KNOWING YOUR COMMUNITY

Do you know your community? Do you know interesting places to go and interesting things to do in your own neighborhood? Here are three short stories about boys and girls who found out how to have good times in their communities.

Early one spring the Scout leader put a notice on the school board. This was the notice Ben read:

Nature Walk

Saturday morning—
Meet at the school at seven o'clock.
Bring your breakfast.
Old and young invited!

On Saturday morning Ben and his father came to school. They found thirty others already there— boys and girls, teachers, fathers and mothers, and the Scout leader.

They all walked down the road to the woods and then turned into a little path. They went along quietly, looking and listening. A red-winged blackbird flashed by, and Ben heard its whistle several times. He saw skunk cabbage in every wet spot.

"Why, here's my old friend Jack," said Ben's father, laughing. He showed Ben a green flower with dark purple stripes. That was a jack-in-the-pulpit, one of the earliest spring flowers.

At eight o'clock they climbed a little hill and sat on some large flat rocks to eat their breakfast. While he ate an orange and an egg sandwich and drank the hot chocolate his mother had put in a thermos * bottle, Ben learned something about rocks. Ben's father said the stones they were sitting on were very, very old.

"If they could talk, they would have an interesting story to tell," he said. "Look at these marks on them. They were made by a great sheet of ice that covered the land long ago. It's hard to believe now, but at one time this community of ours was buried under tons and tons of ice."

Ben had not thought that an early morning walk could be such an adventure. As he walked back with the others, he felt like an explorer who had just discovered a new world. Ben decided to join the Scouts so that he would have more good adventures.

One day the librarian from the town library came to Betty's class. The librarian brought some new books with her and read aloud from them.

There was one story about two children who were roasting potatoes in tin cans in a vacant lot. When a rags-and-bottle man came along, they shared their picnic lunch with him. He told them stories of the treasures he had found among the old rags and bottles. Betty wanted to read more outdoor stories.

Before the librarian left, she invited all the boys and girls to come to the library. She told them that they could each have a library card of their own. With a card a boy or girl could take out any of the books she had shown them and many more besides. All the boys and girls had to do was keep the books clean and bring them back on time.

Betty took out her library card that very afternoon. She was lucky enough to find a book she had been wanting to read. Since that first day she has taken out many books. She has found that the library in her community is a treasure house.

Nancy decided that the church is a community treasure house, too. She had always liked to go to church on Sundays. She liked to see the light shining through the colored glass windows and to listen to the organ music. She liked the talk that was given for the children. After she had been to church she always felt rested.

When Nancy joined the Girl Scouts, she learned that the church helped the community on other days besides Sunday. Friday afternoons the Scout troop held their meetings in the basement. One day they set the table for a church supper. Another day they made up a play showing the kinds of work their fathers did. Mary's father was a policeman. David's father was a painter. Ben's father was a postman. Each of the fathers helped in some way to make the community better. The Scouts did many things for health and safety. They raised vegetables. They took care of small children. They helped to make their homes and community safer.

One Saturday the Scouts in Nancy's troop took a trip through the city. They visited the museum, the library, the parks, and other interesting places. It was fun to work and play with others in the community. Nancy was very happy in her Scout troop and glad that the church had given them such a good meeting place.

SCHOOL SPIRIT

The school is a little community inside the big community where people live. Boys and girls spend a large part of every day in this small community. In fact, the schools really belong to the boys and girls who live in them. If they like, they can make their school community better and safer in many ways.

In one school the children decided that they did not like the muddy yard in front of their school building. So they planted grass seed and put flower seed at each edge of the walk. It was not long before the yard was one of the prettiest school yards you ever saw.

Which?

Which of these boys and girls would you put on a "Good Citizen" list?

1. Bob went down the street eating a banana. He threw the peel on the sidewalk.

2. Betty often went to the park to look at the beautiful flowers. She never picked any of them.

3. Robert cleaned the snow off the sidewalk in front of his house right after every snowstorm.

4. Frank stole a sign that said "Scarlet Fever" from the front of a house that he passed. He tacked it on his chum's house to tease him.

5. Ellen dropped a milk bottle on the sidewalk as she was going to the store. She was in such a hurry that she did not take time to pick up the pieces of glass.

6. Dick helped his father mend and paint the old fence around their yard and to plant a garden.

7. Ruth saw a little child who was crying because he was lost. She talked to him until she found out his name and where he lived. She took him home.

8. Ted helped to raise money for a community playground. It was to be built in memory of the men who were killed in World War II.

WHY IS THIS BOY A GOOD CITIZEN?

Things to Think About

1. Do we have to be old enough to vote before we can be good citizens?
2. What does "community spirit" mean? What does "school spirit" mean?

Things to Do

1. What do you think a good citizen of your community should do? Add your ideas to those of other children in your class.
2. Write and give a play about a boy who was not a good citizen but who became one after he learned more about his town. The play that you write might be like this:

>I. Jack carves his initial on a beautiful tree in the park. He leaves food and papers on the grass there. He laughs as his friends clean up the picnic place.
>
>II. Jack's cousins come to visit. They like the pretty town and its beautiful park. They ask Jack to show them the whole town. Jack sees parts of the town where people do not seem to care how things look.
>
>III. Jack learns about a boys' club that works to clean ugly, vacant lots and make them into pretty places where children like to play. He joins the club and helps with the work.

3. Make a scrapbook of pictures showing men, women, and children making their town safer, cleaner, and more beautiful.
4. Make a model of your community. Put in all the good places to play, the library, churches, and other places of interest.
5. In a class meeting tell how you think your school can be made more attractive.

HEALTH SPIRIT

Part of community spirit and school spirit is health spirit. Health spirit is shown in many ways. One of these ways is by keeping germs in their place. This is a good way for our own health and for others' health. In the first unit you learned a little about germs—bacteria and viruses. Here are more ways of keeping germs from spreading.

Going to school when we do not feel well is one way of spreading germs. But germs may be spread in many other ways. Sometimes we spread them by our bad health habits. Do you know the bad habit that is most common among boys and girls? It is the habit of putting fingers, pens, pencils, and other objects in the mouth. Did you guess it? Perhaps you guessed that sneezing and coughing without covering the mouth is most common. If you did, you were almost right, because that habit is common, too.

Germs can get on your pencil in a number of ways. Just think of all the places where your pencil might have been. Somebody might have sneezed above your pencil or even put it in his mouth. You might have dropped your pencil on the floor or touched the point of it with dirty hands. It might have touched a dirty handkerchief in your pocket. Flies that had been in dirty places might have wiped their feet on it. In these ways germs that cause colds, diphtheria, measles, scarlet fever, typhoid fever, and many other diseases may be spread.

The best way to keep germs in their place is to keep them out of our own bodies. There are just three things we should put in our mouths—our toothbrushes and clean food and water. Food that has been partly eaten by another person is not fit for us to eat. Water in glasses other people have used is not safe water for us to drink.

Soap and warm water, by keeping us clean, help to keep germs in their place. To keep ourselves clean, we need warm water for washing and cool water for rinsing, and we need pure, mild soap.

Do you wash your hands with soap before eating and after using the toilet and before going to bed? Germs die more quickly on a clean skin than on a dirty skin. Dirty hands often carry germs that cause disease. From the hands germs and dirt get on our food. Just think in how many dirty places your hands have been during a morning.

When germs cannot get into our bodies through our mouths, they sometimes try to get in through our skin. But germs cannot enter a skin that has no breaks in it. If we do have an open place in our skin, we should have it taken care of right away. Any scratch, blister, cut, or other break in the skin should be cleaned with alcohol, then covered with sterile gauze.*

Keeping germs out of our own bodies is not enough to stop the spread of germs. We must do all we can to keep germs out of other people's bodies.

We must always cover our nose and mouth when we sneeze. When we have any disease that is catching, we must stay at home. Also we must take care that other people in our own family do not catch any sickness from us. Using our own towel and washcloth and washing our hands often help to keep other people well when we are sick.

To keep ourselves and other children well, our school must be clean. Boys and girls can do a great deal to help keep the school clean. They can keep their own things picked up and put away in the places where they belong. They can help keep all books clean. They can turn the pages of a book without wetting their fingers. Certainly it is not pleasant for other people to handle books that someone has spit on—for that is what you have done when you wet your fingers and then turn the pages.

Peggy's class had been talking about some of the ways to keep from spreading germs. They knew many of the ways that you have just read about:

1. Keeping things out of the mouth
2. Having clean food and water
3. Keeping ourselves clean
4. Keeping the school clean

"Who can think of other ways to put germs in their place?" Miss Winter asked.

"When I sweep the kitchen for Mother," said Peggy, "I make sure that there is no uncovered food in the kitchen. I scatter small pieces of damp newspaper around. That keeps the dust from flying all over everything."

"That is the way to sweep," said Miss Winter. "When you use a dust mop, do you put a little water or oil on it? That keeps the dust from flying, too. There may be harmful germs in dust."

"That's what Mother says," said Peggy. "So I shake the dust mop and dustcloth in the sunshine. I wash them, too, so that they will not be full of germs all the time."

"Sunshine is our cheapest and best germ killer. The rooms of our homes and our school should be as full of sunshine as possible. We ourselves should spend several hours a day outdoors in the sunshine," Miss Winter told them.

"I've just made up a poem about germs," said Sam, with a grin.

"Will you read it to us?" asked Miss Winter.

This is what Sam read:

> "The germs give up
> And lose all hope
> When they meet sun,
> Or fire, or soap."

The children all laughed. Miss Winter said, "That is a good poem to remember. Sunshine, fire, and soap can do a great deal to get rid of disease germs."

The boys and girls all decided that they would try to have sunshine indoors and out of doors, to burn up rubbish, and to wash their hands often. They thought that building good health habits would be the best way to show their health spirit.

Other Children's Questions

What are the right answers to these questions, which other children have asked?

1. Why do we have to wash our hands before eating?
2. Why should we keep our schoolbooks clean?

Find the Right Word

Here are some sentences in which words are missing. Find the right word for each blank. The words are: sunshine, alcohol, towel, washed, used, covered, dirty. (Do not write in this book.)

1. Food kept from one meal to another should be kept clean and ———.
2. One boy's whistle should not be ——— by another boy.
3. Our hands should be ——— before every meal.
4. Three good germ killers are ———, fire, and soap.
5. A cut or scratch should be cleaned with ———.
6. Each person should use his own washcloth and ———.
7. Flies carry germs on their feet, because they walk in ——— places.

Things to Think About

1. Are all germs bad?
2. What are other names for some kinds of germs?
3. Why is it selfish to go to school when you have a sore throat and headache?
4. How do we help our community when we prevent germs from spreading?

Things to Do

1. If you begin to get a sore throat, running nose, or rash during school hours, tell the teacher at once. If you do so, you may prevent other children from catching a cold or some other disease.

2. Make a scrapbook called "Stopping the Germ Parade." In it put pictures of children bathing, washing their hands, sneezing into handkerchiefs, staying in bed with a cold, helping keep a room at home or at school clean, and doing other things to keep germs from spreading.

3. Make posters that show how to keep diseases from spreading. Some of these posters might show

   (1) a man putting a screen in a kitchen window.
   (2) a doctor washing his hands before he examines a child.
   (3) a mother pouring boiling water over dishes that have been washed in soapsuds.

4. Try to write a poem as good as Sam's about helping others to keep well.

5. Look back over this unit and add the starred words to your dictionary.

6. Look at the picture below. What is the girl in the picture doing to keep germs from spreading? What other health habit do you think she has formed?

Unit IX

ACCIDENTS NEED NOT HAPPEN

"Accidents will happen," people say. Do you think this is true? Another saying is, "Better be safe than sorry." Which saying is the one you use? Read the story about Uncle Jim's first-aid * cupboard to find out whether the boys and girls in the story were "safe" or "sorry." Could the accidents have been prevented? How?

WATERPROOF
ADHESIVE PLASTER
ABSORBENT
HALF POUND NET WEIGHT
BAKING SODA
BICARBONATE OF SODA
STERIPAD
Rubbing Alcohol Compound
Boston · St. Louis
U.S.A.
Solution
Boric Acid
N.F.

THE FIRST-AID CUPBOARD

On the first floor of every home there should be a first-aid cupboard. The cupboard should contain these things:

1. Sterile gauze
2. Bandages
3. Adhesive tape
4. A package of sterile cotton
5. A large bottle of rubbing alcohol
6. A bottle of boric * acid solution
7. A bottle of iodine
8. A jar or tube of petroleum * jelly
9. A package of baking * soda
10. An eye dropper
11. Some needles

All children should know certain simple first-aid rules and helps. To do the right thing at the right time is sometimes a matter of life and death.

It is also important to know what *not* to do. Many lives are lost because first-aiders move a person who is badly hurt. If you are with someone who is badly hurt, do these three things:

1. Leave him where he is, lying down. Do not move him unless he is in danger of further injury.
2. Cover him with blankets or coats.
3. Send or go for help at once. Some person should stay with him if possible.

You can learn how to treat different common kinds of injury. This story tells how Uncle Jim gave first aid to the six cousins he had invited to spend a week with him in his big mountain cabin.

During the week that the six children stayed with their Uncle Jim, everything he had in his first-aid cupboard was used at some time. Uncle Jim knew that there might be many small injuries during the week. But he did not know that he would have to be doctor and nurse as much as he did.

The very first evening Sally did not look where she was going and ran, bump! into a tree. That bump caused a nosebleed. Uncle Jim had her lie down with a cold, wet cloth on her nose. He put another cold, wet cloth at the back of her neck. He told her not to blow her nose for several hours.

The next morning Jack was showing off with his new knife. Instead of using good form and cutting away from him, he cut toward his hand. The knife slipped and cut his thumb. Uncle Jim washed the cut with sterile cotton dipped in alcohol. He did this to kill germs; dead germs can do no harm. Uncle Jim also used the alcohol to kill the germs on the skin around the cut. Live germs in a cut often make it red and sore and may keep it from healing. After cleaning around the wound Uncle Jim covered it with a piece of sterile gauze and bandaged it as in the picture on page 191.

Jean helped cook dinner the second night. She spilled some very hot water on her hand. That place on her hand became quite red. Uncle Jim put petroleum jelly on the red place, wrapped some sterile

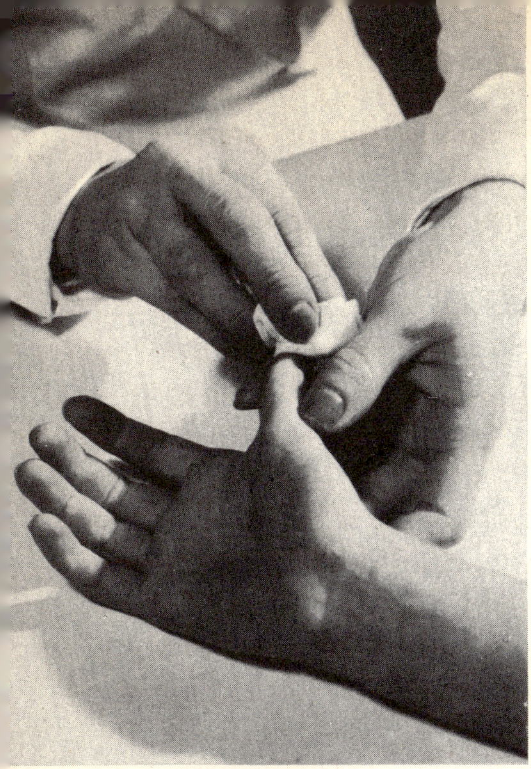

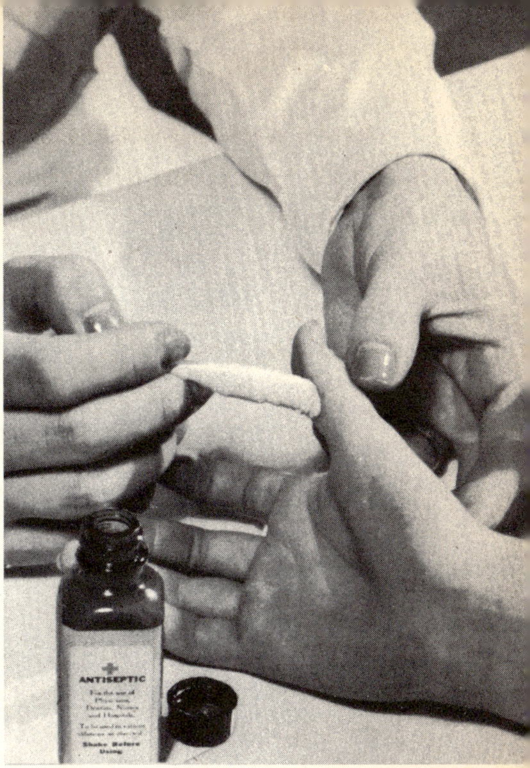
ANTISEPTIC
Shake Before Using

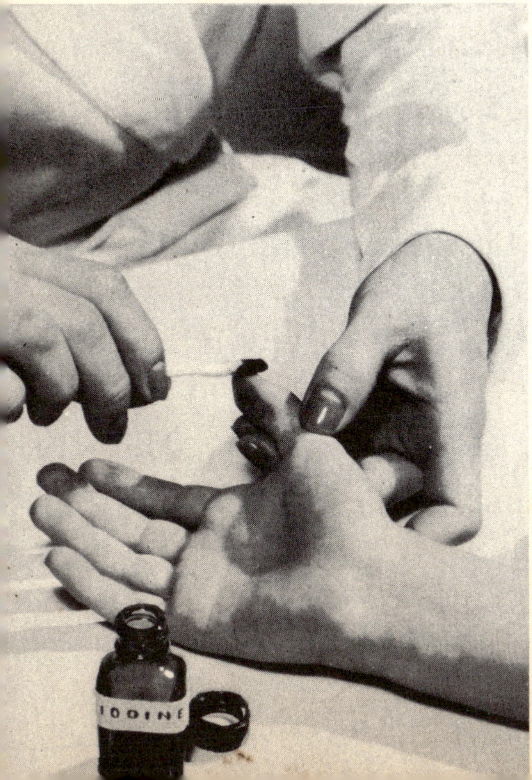
IODINE

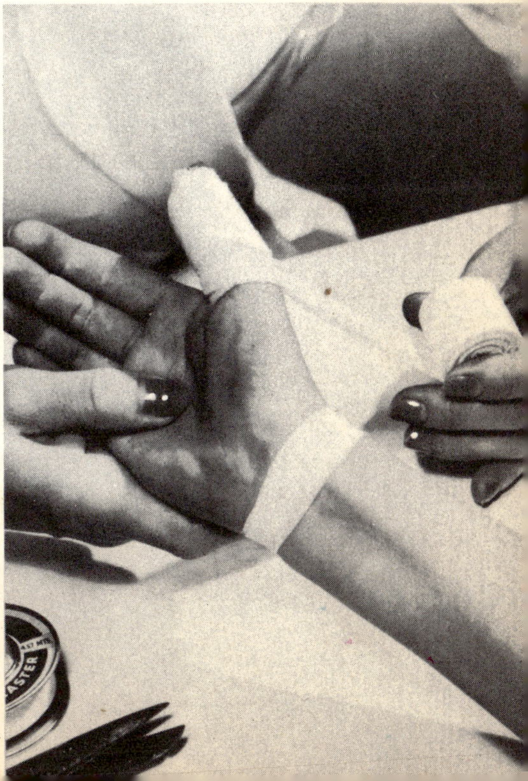

gauze lightly around Jean's hand, and told her to keep that hand dry. He wanted her to keep it clean without having a tight bandage on it. Burns need to be open to the air.

The third day Sam stumbled over a rock and rolled a little way down a steep hill. The fall had bruised * his legs. Uncle Jim took Sam back to the cabin and told him to lie down. He put cold, wet cloths on the bruises.

"If the bruises were already black and blue," he said, "I would put on hot, wet cloths instead of cold, wet cloths."

Late in the afternoon something happened to Sally that was not her fault. A tiny fly got into her eye. It did not feel tiny to Sally.

"Don't rub your eye," Uncle Jim told her. "We can easily wash the fly out."

He got the eye dropper and the boric acid solution. Sally held her head back while Uncle Jim let the boric acid solution run over her eye. In a minute or two the fly was washed out.

The fourth day Bob came back from a long hike with red, itching * hands.

"You must have got into poison * ivy," said Uncle Jim.

He washed Bob's hands with yellow soap and water, put alcohol on them, and then wrapped the itching hands with bandages soaked in baking soda and water.

"Whatever you do, don't scratch," he said to Bob.

"You do not want to spread this rash to other parts of your body."

Dick had been on a long hike. He came back with blisters on both his heels. Uncle Jim put a dot of iodine on the blisters. Then at that spot he opened them with a needle that he had first dipped in alcohol. Next he covered the blisters with pieces of sterile gauze fastened in place with adhesive tape.

That night Sally got a big splinter under one of her fingernails. Uncle Jim pulled the splinter out with a needle that had been made safe by holding it over a flame. "Flame is as good as alcohol to kill the germs on a needle," he said. He put iodine on the hole left by the splinter and then wrapped the finger in sterile gauze held on by adhesive tape.

"You are Dr. Jim," said Sally, laughing. "We keep you busy patching us up."

After that the six children called their uncle Dr. Jim.

The morning of the fifth day Dick and Jack ran into the cabin, shouting about something.

"Did you see bears?" asked Uncle Jim.

"No, we met bees!" cried Dick. "I have two stings and Jack has three."

Uncle Jim put baking soda on the bee stings. Then he bandaged and wet the parts. "Try not to scratch," he said. "You may scratch germs into the sore places." Soon the bee stings did not hurt any more.

On the same day Bob fell from a tree. He had

HOW TO TREAT
A SPRAINED
ANKLE

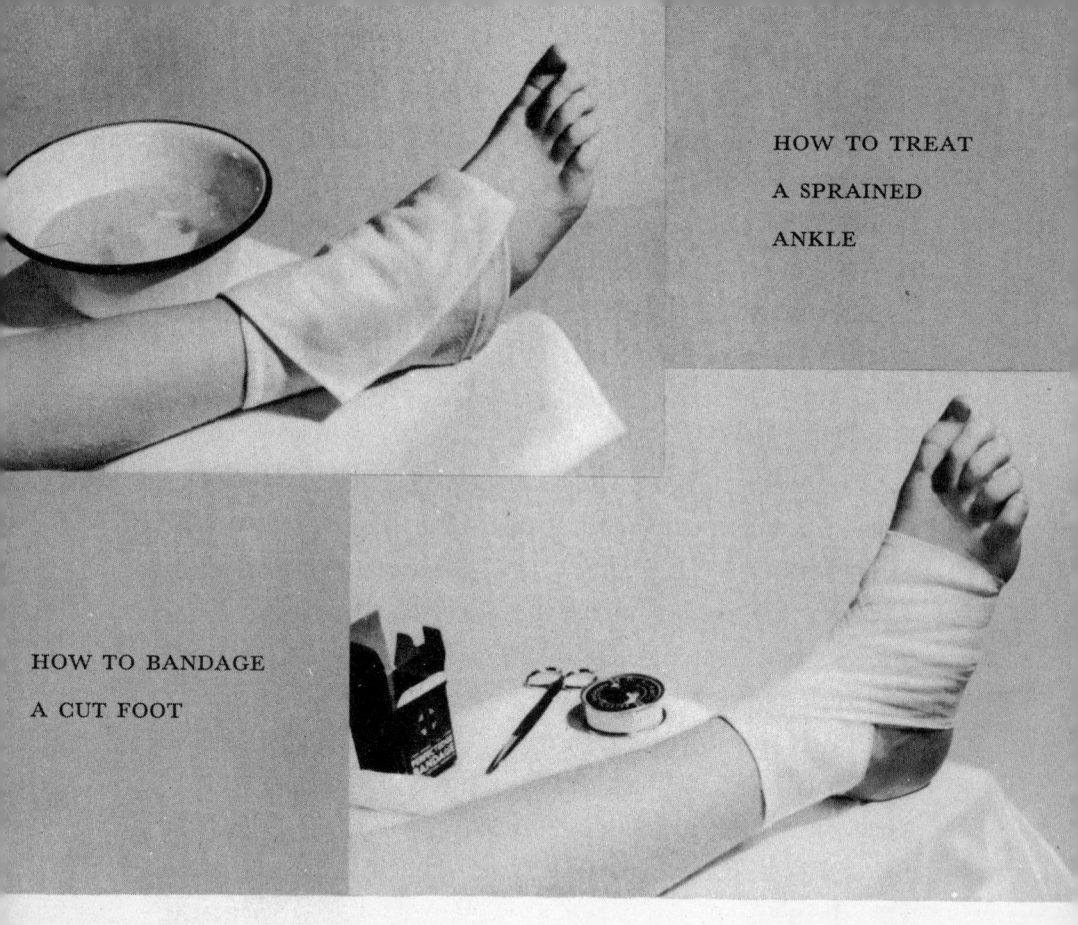

HOW TO BANDAGE
A CUT FOOT

been holding on with two hands, but a branch broke and down he came. His ankle was sprained.* Sam and Uncle Jim carried him to the cabin and laid him on a bed. They raised his foot by putting a large pillow under it. Uncle Jim put a cold, wet cloth on Bob's ankle. Sally said that she wanted to play nurse. She wet the cloth in cold water every few minutes, and then she put it back on Bob's ankle. She did this for two hours.

Uncle Jim called all the children together. He said: "Bob can't walk for a day or so. He must stay off that ankle. I want you to take turns in helping to take care of Bob. Also I want you all to be more careful. Most of these accidents have been due to carelessness. I don't want to play doctor or nurse half the time."

"If Bob had broken his leg instead of spraining his ankle, what would you have done, Dr. Jim?" asked Sally.

"I would have gone to him wherever he was. A person with a broken bone should not be moved until splints * are put around the break. If the bone had not pushed through the skin, I would have made some splints of small boards. I would have padded the splints with cloth to prevent pressure and laid them along his leg. Then I would have tied them on—not too tightly—with a bandage. Sam and Jack would have helped me carry him back to the cabin and put him on a bed. Then I would have telephoned to town for a doctor. If I was not able to get a doctor to come up here at once, I would have taken him to town in my car."

"That would have been a very serious accident," said Dick. "It would have spoiled all our fun for a while, too."

"Yes, accidents always spoil the fun," said Uncle Jim. "And even small injuries can become serious. Any injury should be given good care so that it will not become serious. As it is, my first-aid cupboard has served all our needs. But I've played doctor long enough, and besides my gauze is going to be all gone unless you boys and girls are careful from now on."

"We will be careful," cried the children.

"We've learned a great deal about first aid from you, Dr. Jim," said Sally.

"I'm glad you have," said Uncle Jim, "but it is best to be so careful that you will not need first aid."

Every school should have in a first-aid cupboard the things listed on page 189. Does your school have them?

Things to Do

Tell how each of these injuries should be treated:
1. John has stepped on a piece of glass. His foot is cut and is bleeding a little.
2. Mary has bumped her arm on a stove. There is a red spot near her elbow.
3. Anne has six mosquito bites that itch badly.
4. Barbara has sprained her wrist and bruised her arm.
5. Alice has picked poison ivy by mistake. There is a rash on one hand.
6. Jim has fallen from the porch and broken his arm.
7. Dorothy has a blister on her heel.

SAFETY ON THE STREET AND ROAD

Crossing streets is something we do every day. Here are things to do if we are to cross safely:

1. Cross only at the corner crossings. Never "jay-walk," or cross at any other places. Car drivers must move rather fast between crossings or they will get

in the way of other cars. They expect to stop at crossings or look out there for persons walking across the street.

2. Before crossing, wait until cars near at hand have stopped or until no cars are near. Look both ways as you are crossing.

You have to look out for yourself because we have many dangerous drivers on the road. Some drivers do not see well; some have been having alcoholic drinks; some are careless and thoughtless. When we are walking, we must remember to look out for such drivers; they will not look out for us.

Have you ever watched a chipmunk or a squirrel? How often they stop, look, and listen! Perhaps you have seen a chipmunk first stick its nose out of its hole and wait a half minute or more. Then it comes out farther, waits again, and looks in every direction. Are you as careful when your ball rolls into the road or when you cross the street?

3. Move when the green light says, "Go." Wait when the red light says, "Wait." Obey the traffic signs and officer.

Here are three more rules for safety:

1. Never play in a street that cars pass through.
2. Look out for the safety of younger children in the street and in the road.
3. Always walk on the left side of a country road. Step out of the road as the cars come past.

We are safe when we "stop, look, and listen"; when we "watch our step"; when we "keep our wits about us"; and when we learn to do quickly what our ears and eyes tell us to do.

STREETCARS AND BUSES

Many children have to go to school on streetcars or buses. There are several things to remember about streetcar and bus safety.

1. Never get on or off a streetcar or bus while it is moving.

2. When getting on or off, face forward, hold on with the left hand, watch the steps.

3. Look out for passing cars as you get off a streetcar or bus. Stay in the safety zone, if there is one, until the way is clear. Then you can walk safely to the sidewalk.

4. When you are on a streetcar or bus, do not stick your head or hands out of the window. You can see why to do so is dangerous.

RAILROADS

If you have to cross railroad tracks, remember:

1. Stop and listen and look both ways before you cross.

2. Cross only at the regular crossings.

3. Never cross when the bars or gates are down because a train is coming.

4. Do not walk on the rails or tracks.

5. Never go between the cars of a train that has stopped. Never get on the cars "for fun." Railroad yards and stations are not places to play.

School children are learning to prevent accidents by obeying the laws of safety. In one year recently in the United States the number of children killed by automobiles was less than it was ten years before. If everyone is careful, fewer children will be killed by automobiles in the next five years.

Which Is Wise? Which Is Foolish?

Read these foolish and wise things that children have done. Which are the foolish things to do? Which are the wise things to do?

1. Bob had only three minutes to go five blocks to school. He ran all the way, not looking to left or right or waiting for cars to pass at the crossings.

2. Jim never crossed a street when there was a red light. He always waited for the green light.

3. Mary lived right across the street from a store. When she went to the store on an errand, she walked up to the corner and crossed at the crossing.

4. Bob, Bill, and Dick played ball every afternoon in the middle of a busy street.

5. David always rode his bicycle near the curb at the right side of the street.

6. Alice never turned a corner on her bicycle without first making a sign with her hand.

7. Agnes and Sally walked along a country road to school. They walked on the right, not the left, side of the road. They did not mind having cars come up behind them.

Things to Think About

1. Why is a boy or girl who is careless a poor sport?
2. Explain how safety and good times go together.

Things to Do

1. Give a play to children in the lower grades which will show them how to cross a street safely, how to walk safely on a country road, and how to step off a streetcar or bus safely. Teach them that it is foolish—not smart—to take chances.

2. Have a poster show. Let the posters tell about safety on streets and roads. Some of the posters might show

(1) where to walk across a street.
(2) how to walk on a country road.
(3) how to get off a streetcar or bus.

3. Have a safety club. Meet in school or in your own homes. Choose a name for the club. Each member should practice safety rules during the week and tell at the meeting about some act of safety.

SAFE OUTDOOR PLAY

"Oh, I didn't mean to hurt you. I'm so sorry!"

You have often heard these words on the playground. And you have sometimes seen the bleeding nose or the bad bump or the scratched arm which shows that somebody did not think what he was doing or watch where he was going. It is "better to be safe than sorry."

What kinds of accidents have you or your friends had when you were playing after school or at recess? Discuss in class some of these accidents, telling the causes and the results of each. Then tell how each might have been prevented. Here are accidents that happened to some schoolboys and schoolgirls:

One day Jim was playing on the school swing. He stood up in the seat. He did not bother to hold onto the ropes tightly. The board slipped. Jim fell and broke his right arm. For weeks he could not write; he could not play ball; he could not steer his bicycle.

Tom hurt his arm and cut his head when he fell off his bicycle. Why did he fall? He knew how to ride. He had had no falls while he was learning. He was very careful then. He fell the day he was chasing automobiles, holding onto the backs of wagons, and not looking where he was going. A dozen times he just missed being hurt. It was a stone in the road that finally caused the accident. He could have steered around it if he had seen it in time, but he was riding too fast. Crash! Tom and his bicycle landed in a heap. The front wheel was bent out of shape. Tom felt bent out of shape, too. Luckily he had no broken bones, but he had many cuts and bruises.

His mother was frightened when she saw him; and when his father heard about the accident, he said: "Well, Tom, when I got you that bicycle I thought you were old enough to know how to ride safely. It will be a long time before you have another."

Now Tom walks to school. As he starts out he often thinks: "I wish I'd played safe. Then I wouldn't have to be sorry now."

Mary tripped on a shoelace when she was running. She fell on the sidewalk and skinned her knee badly. "I knew I should have tied that shoelace tight," she thought.

Fred always got excited when he was playing

games. One day he ran into Jim and knocked him down. "I'm very sorry," he said. "I should have looked where I was going." Of course Fred was sorry, but that didn't help Jim. He had knocked out part of a front tooth when he fell.

Bill fell on a sharp stone, which made a bad cut over his eye. "We should not have left sticks and stones and boards with nails in them lying around on the playground," he said. As soon as the doctor had treated the cut, Bill came back to the playground and began to pick up the sticks and stones. He looked for nails that were sticking up from boards; he pulled out the nails or bent them into the wood with a hammer and then put the nails and the boards away in a safe place.

A stray cat scratched Tony when he was playing with it. The cat did not think Tony's rough handling was play. If Tony had thought ahead, he would not have played with the cat in just that way. Tony soon learned not to go near strange cats and dogs even though they seemed friendly.

Cats, dogs, and other animals get into all kinds of places. Some of these places are very dirty. Their fur has more germs on it than dirty hands have. That is why Alice always washes her hands after she has been playing with a cat or dog.

Bill liked to climb trees. He chose his trees carefully. He did not climb trees with dead branches. But one day he fell from a tree because his hand slipped off the branch. He got a big bump on his head. After that he followed this rule: Always hold on in two places. This rule worked very well. If one hand slipped, he held fast with the other hand. If both hands slipped, he still had a firm hold with his legs. Using this rule, Bill never fell out of trees again. Climbing trees takes skill and care.

If you like climbing trees, be sure
    You grip *two* places well
With hands *and* feet to be secure.
    Remember careless friends who fell.

Helen saw some little children chasing one another with rough, pointed sticks in their hands. Helen called the children to her. She showed them a good place to lay their sticks while they were playing. She also showed them how to carry the sticks with the points down.

Things to Do

1. When you play, practice all the ways you have learned to keep accidents from spoiling the fun.

2. Try to play out of doors for about two hours every day and always use good form in every game.

3. Make a list of ways for ball players to use good form, such as: Drop your bat at your feet when you start to run to first base—do not throw it away from you.

4. Do you go roller skating? Why is it not wise for many children to roller skate to school? Where are safe places to skate near your home and school? Why is it dangerous to skate after dark? Make a list of all the ways in which you can prevent accidents when you are roller skating. Show your list to other children in the class and ask them to let you see their lists. Check on your list all the safe things you will be sure to do if you go skating this afternoon.

5. What should you do for safety if

(1) you have been eating a banana out of doors?
(2) you want to make a slide in the snow?
(3) you are waiting in line or are in a crowd?
(4) you are walking in the dark?
(5) you are walking on streets where men have been working?
(6) you are swinging?
(7) you have a bicycle?
(8) you see sharp stones or boards with nails on the playground?
(9) you are climbing a tree?
(10) you meet a stray animal?
(11) you are carrying a pointed stick or other sharp object?
(12) you see that it has been snowing?

Write the answers to these questions in your notebook.

SAFETY IN SCHOOL

Have you had any accidents in your school? What were they? Where did they happen? How do you think they could have been prevented?

Read this story to see if you think Bob prevented an accident.

Bob was a member of the Safety Council in his school. He was elected by his class because he kept the school rules himself and did his best to get others to keep them. He was willing to give up part of his playtime to help make his school better and safer.

Bob was in charge of the main hall and stairway. He helped to teach the boys and girls to walk on the right-hand side of the halls and stairs. That was the first rule that the Safety Council had made. "No running" and "No pushing" were two other rules they made later.

One day Bob saw his best friend Charles running down the stairs. Charles did not see the first-grade child coming up until he bumped right into her. She was not badly hurt, but Bob knew that she might have been. He had spoken to Charles before about running on the stairs and in the halls. He had said, "If it happens again, Charles, I'll have to report you to the Safety Council." Now it had happened. Bob hated to report his best friend, but he had to keep the school safe for all the pupils. So Charles was reported.

When Charles came before the Safety Council, the president said, "Do you know why you were asked to come before the Safety Council?"

"Yes," said Charles. "I was running and Bob reported me. That shows Bob was on the job."

The Council liked the way Charles admitted that he was wrong and that Bob was right. They gave him a high mark for that.

"Why were you running, Charles?" the president asked. "Were you late?"

"No," Charles answered, "I had plenty of time."

"Did you want to catch up with someone?"

"No."

"Then why did you run?"

"I don't know really. I guess it was because it's exciting to run downstairs."

Everyone laughed and Charles laughed with them.

"It wouldn't seem so funny if you had really hurt that little girl. I know you're sorry you bumped her, but you must learn to be careful. The next time you come downstairs, count each step slowly to remind yourself not to run. And, if you are looking for excitement, ask Mr. Hall to let you do some safe stunts in the gym."

Charles did as the president of the Safety Council told him. Never again did anyone have to report him for running down the stairs or in the hall.

SAFETY IN THE HOME

How many secrets of preventing accidents at school, on the street, and at home have you discovered? See how many more you can learn from these pages.

STORIES OF FALLS

In the home many children—and older people, too—have falls. In some cases, like Humpty Dumpty, they cannot be put together again. In every case the fall is painful and prevents a person from doing what he wants to do. The following stories tell about accidents that might have been prevented.

Betty was late going to bed. She was late getting up the next morning. She was late getting ready for school. At last she was ready. She started down the front stairs, two steps at a time. She slipped near the top and fell right down to the bottom. She hurt herself so badly that she had to stay in bed all week.

"It would have been better to be careful and be a minute late than to miss a whole week of school," she said. "After this I'm going to bed on time so that I'll get up in time and not have to hurry."

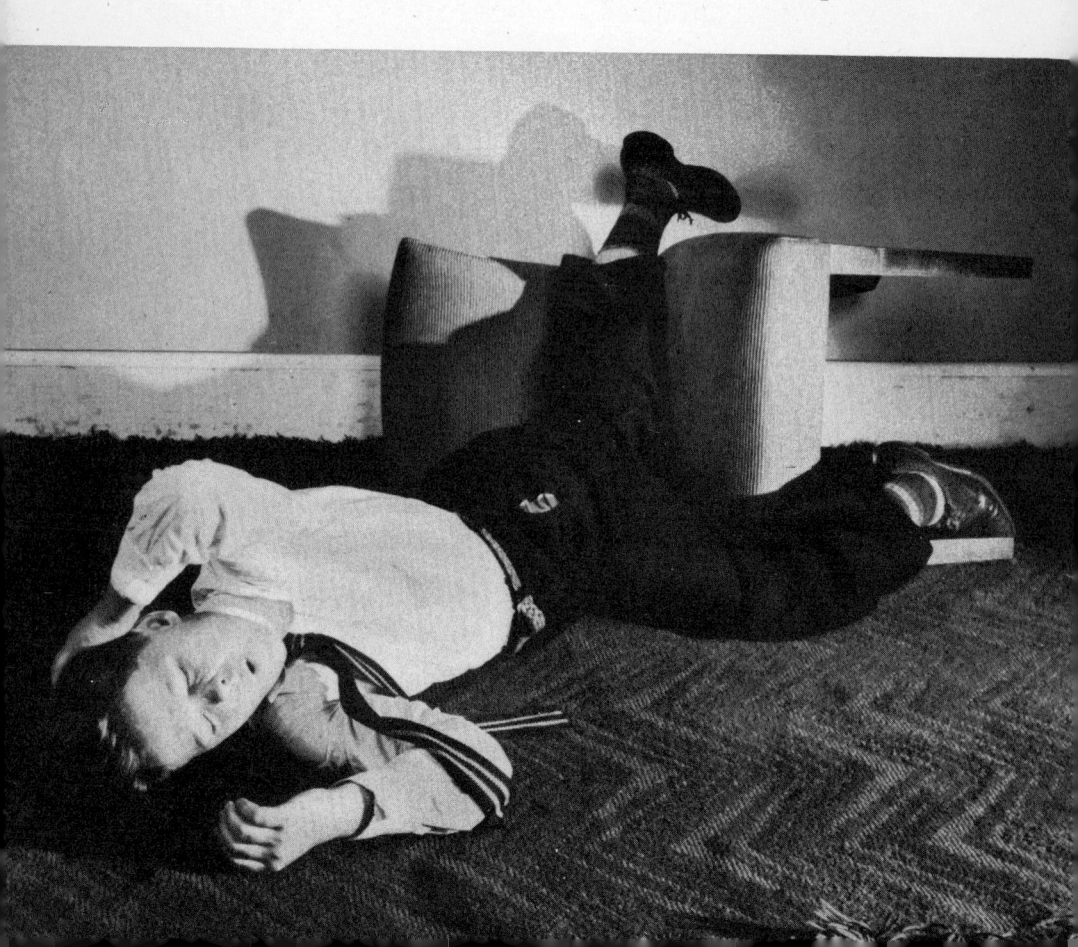

When Bobby was running from one room to another in the dark, he fell over a chair that he himself had left in the middle of his path. A small bone in his foot was broken. He could not go to camp until several weeks later than he had planned to go. When he did go, he still had to be careful of his foot. He could not play the games he liked best to play.

He wished that he had put the chair back in its place. His mother had told him many times to keep things out of people's way, and he always was careful with his toys and tools. She had said, too, that it is very dangerous to leave anything on the stairs or at the top or the bottom of a flight of steps. He would remember now and be careful so that no one else would have an accident through his fault.

Dorothy's baby brother fell out of the window when he was leaning against the screen. Luckily it was a first-floor window, and he was not badly hurt. Accidents of this kind can be prevented by fastening the screen firmly or by opening the upper part of the window, leaving the lower part closed.

Mary's mother caught her foot in a hole in the carpet when she was coming downstairs with a tray of dishes in her hands. She fell to the bottom of the stairs and was under the doctor's care for weeks. How might this accident have been prevented? Safe stairs should have: (1) a handrail which a person can take hold of when he comes downstairs; (2) a carpet free from holes; and (3), if possible, an electric light that can be turned on at either the top or the bottom of the stairs.

Charlie fell when he was trying to reach his baseball glove on the top shelf of the closet. He had piled boxes on top of one another, and they fell apart after he had climbed to the top. A stepladder should be used instead of boxes, barrels, and rocking chairs. It should be set firmly on the floor. The person using the stepladder should not lean too far in any direction.

Most of the falls at home are of the following kinds: falls on wet or slippery floors, falls on small rugs, falls over stools or other objects, falls on steps and stairs; falls from ladders that are not set up firmly and from chairs and boxes used instead of ladders, falls from windows and porches. What could you do to prevent each of these falls?

BURNS, FIRES, AND STOVES

One of the most frequent and painful injuries is a burn. A slight burn makes the skin red and sore. A more severe * burn often causes a blister. In a blister a watery liquid collects between two layers of skin—the upper, outside layer and the layer underneath. In a severe burn the outer layers of the skin are destroyed. Such a burn must be carefully protected from germs. How many of the burns that you or your small brothers and sisters have had might have been prevented? The following short stories tell how some common burns might have been prevented.

Bill was telling his sister about the pet dog they were going to get. He was so excited about the dog that he did not notice where he was going. He ran against the hot stove and burned his arm. How might this burn have been prevented? It is a good plan to draw a "safety zone" around hot stoves and electric irons. This can be made by putting a white line on the floor around the stove or ironing board. The children can be taught to stay outside the white line. It is good to have a "safety zone" when there are very young children in the family. Then there is less danger that they will get burned.

Alice was burned when she was lighting the gas oven. She lighted a match, turned on the gas, and pop!—out jumped a flame. Her mother said: "I should have shown you the right way to light a gas oven. You should open the oven door first, then turn on the gas and hold the lighted match to it. If the match goes out, turn off the gas and begin again."

Mary was standing near her mother while she was cooking potatoes in hot fat. Some of the hot fat spattered on Mary as the pieces of potatoes were dropped into it. There was a little red burn on her arm where each drop of hot fat fell. Four ways of preventing burns from hot fat are: (1) staying away from kettles of hot fat; (2) being careful not to drop water or wet foods into hot fat, because water makes hot fat spatter; (3) putting a cover on the pot; and (4) setting the pot of hot fat away from the edge of the stove.

Jean spilled some boiling-hot chocolate on her hand. The cup was so full that it splashed over as she carried it. "After this I'm going to fill my cup only three quarters full," Jean said.

Sam heard his mother call, "Fire!" He ran into the room and found his mother's dress, the wastebasket, and the curtains on fire. He wrapped a heavy rug around his mother's burning dress from her head down. The rug put out the fire.

By that time the fire in the room had flared up so high that he and his mother did not think they could put it out. His mother went to the telephone and said, "I wish to report a fire." She then gave her address slowly and clearly. Sam at the same time was bringing up pails of water and pouring them on the fire. If there had not been a telephone, he would have had to run to the nearest fire alarm box to send in an alarm. The water that Sam brought kept the fire from spreading, but he could not have put it out without the firemen's help. His mother said: "I did a very foolish thing. I threw a match into the wastebasket without making sure that the match was really out. After this I shall put burnt matches in a little jar."

If oil or kerosene had caught fire, Sam would

not have used water to put out the fire. Water makes oil or kerosene spatter and spreads the fire. But salt, sand, or dirt thrown on the oil or kerosene flames beats them down and puts out the fire.

"Escaping gas!" Helen thought she smelled gas and went to the kitchen at once to see about it, because it is dangerous to inhale gas. She found that the pot on the gas stove had boiled over and put out the fire, but the gas kept coming out into the room. Helen turned off the gas at once and opened the windows. No harm was done. "There is an old saying," said her mother, "that, if you watch a pot, it never boils. It would be truer to say that, if you watch a pot, it need not boil *over*."

HOW TO PREVENT OTHER KINDS OF ACCIDENTS

Electricity is one of our best helpers—if we use it carefully. The right way to take hold of an electric cord is with dry hands. Water on hands or on floors makes a short cut for an electric current. It is a short cut that can kill. So, you see, you should never touch any electric object with wet hands or even when your feet are wet. No electric object should be in reach of a person in the bathtub.

In nearly every house "junk" collects. Old papers, oily rags, broken chairs, and other things left lying around may cause falls and fires. Here is a poem called "Junk":

Our little house holds many things
    That don't go in a trunk,
Unused, or old, or broken things,
    That Mom and Dad call "junk."

They drift to closet and to drawer,
    They pile up on a shelf.
They clutter up the basement floor.
    I think we need an elf.

To take them out and leave us space
    Safely to come and go.
They trap us in, they fill the place;
    They could cause fires, you know.

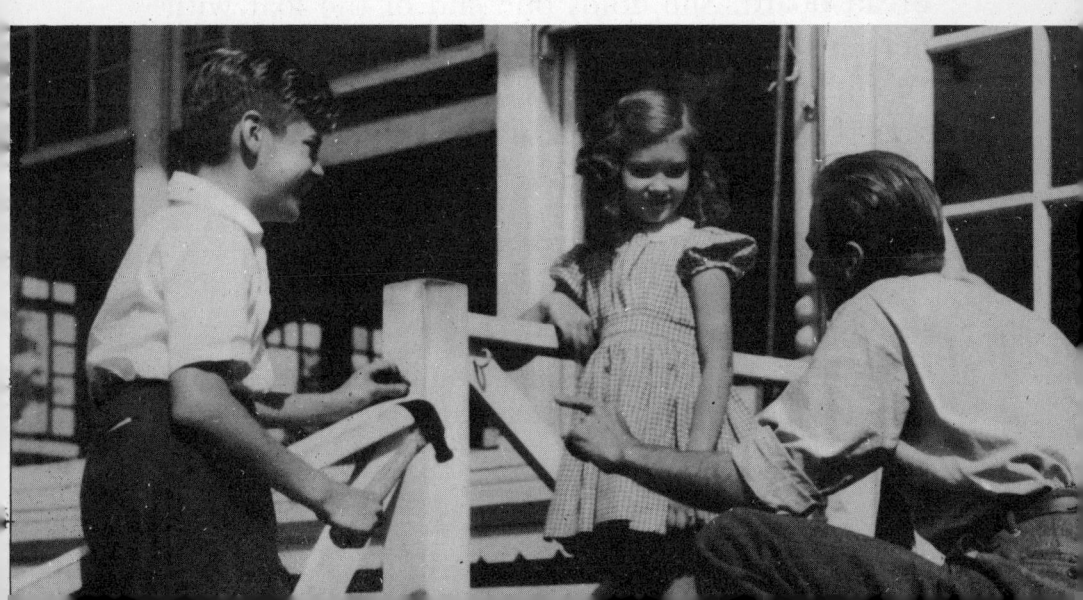

Many accidents in the home happen to small children. They are into everything. They have not yet learned what is safe and what is not safe. Big brothers and sisters should teach little children to play safe. They should put out of reach anything that might hurt them. The following stories tell how to keep little brothers and sisters from getting hurt.

Peggy has a little brother. She keeps all pins, needles, tacks, and nails well out of his reach. She also keeps all sharp things such as knives and scissors in places where he cannot get them. Matches are kept on high shelves. When he grows a little older, Peggy will show her brother how to use matches in the right way. She will teach him to strike the match on the box, to hold the match away from him, and to put it in the glass jar for burnt matches when it has been used.

Anne likes to cut paper dolls. She keeps the points of her scissors stuck in a cork when she carries them about. She gives her five-year-old sister the scissors with round ends.

In cutting bread Mary Ann puts the bread on the bread board. She holds one end of the loaf with her left hand and cuts slices from the other end. In cutting pieces from a stick of wood Jerry cuts away from his body. Jack stands the wood up and holds it with his hand out of the way of danger. Look at the pictures on page 219. If the ax or the knife slipped, could it cut the boy using it?

Which?

Which of these children did not think of other people's safety? Which of these children did?

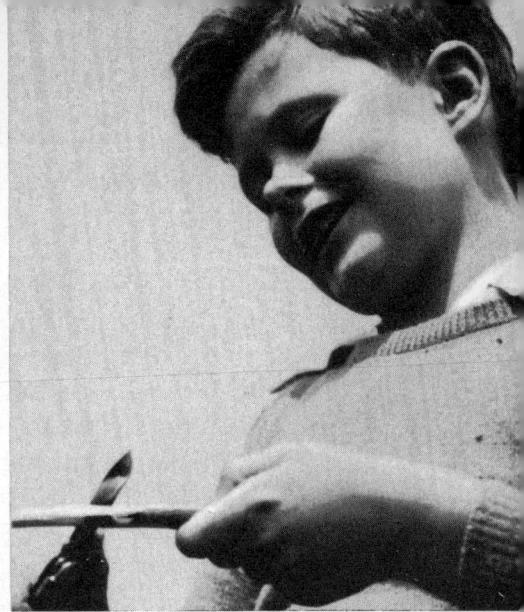

1. Dick peeled a banana as he went upstairs. He dropped the peel on the stairs.

2. Margaret left her doll furniture in the middle of the living room when she went to bed.

3. Bob heard a pan of soup boil over on the gas stove. He ran to the kitchen, turned off the gas, and opened the windows.

4. Jane spilled some gravy on the kitchen floor. She did not bother to wipe it up.

5. Frank left a box of matches on a table. His little brother came into the room as Frank went out.

6. Jean's mother was very busy in the kitchen. Jean's baby sister was playing in the kitchen and getting in her mother's way. Jean took the baby outdoors to play.

7. Bill saw that one of the upstairs screens was loose. He told his father about it at once. Bill was thinking of the safety of his baby brother and a little sister.

Things to Think About

1. Why should you not run if your clothing is on fire? What should you do?

2. How do we happen to have the saying "a safe and sane Fourth of July"? Should we be "safe and sane" only on the Fourth of July?

Things to Do

1. Make a safety exhibit. Find or draw pictures showing how to prevent cuts, scratches, falls, and burns.

2. Read the section about safety in the home to your family. Ask the following questions about your house: Are there piles of papers lying around in the cellar or closets? Are oily rags thrown in a heap in any part of the house? Are ashes put in a wooden or paper box? Are matches left where small children can easily reach them? Are the porch and stairway rails strong? Is the stairway safe? Are there any curtains near gas jets? Is the medicine chest where small children cannot reach it? Find out what is not safe. Then plan ways in which you can prevent falls, burns, and other accidents in your home.

3. Plan several plays for a lower grade showing how children can keep from getting burned. Be sure to include ways to keep from being burned by kettles of hot water or by playing with the gas or with matches.

4. Visit a firehouse in your community. Ask a fireman to tell you what to do to prevent fires. Why are fire drills in school important? How should you act in a fire drill?

5. Look around your schoolroom and playground. See how many things you can find which might cause accidents, such as broken glass, sharp objects lying around, and chairs or anything else out of place. Make changes so that these things can do no harm. In class tell how you helped to make the schoolroom and the playground safe.

6. Teach little children to put their hands on the part of a door and a window where their fingers cannot be caught if the door or window shuts suddenly.

UNIT X

A HAPPY VACATION

Vacation days can be the happiest days of the year; yet every year accidents spoil some vacations. We need to remember our health and safety rules all the time. Some of them are more important in vacation days than they are now.

In this unit you will learn how you can help make your vacation a happy one. You can think about this even before vacation begins.

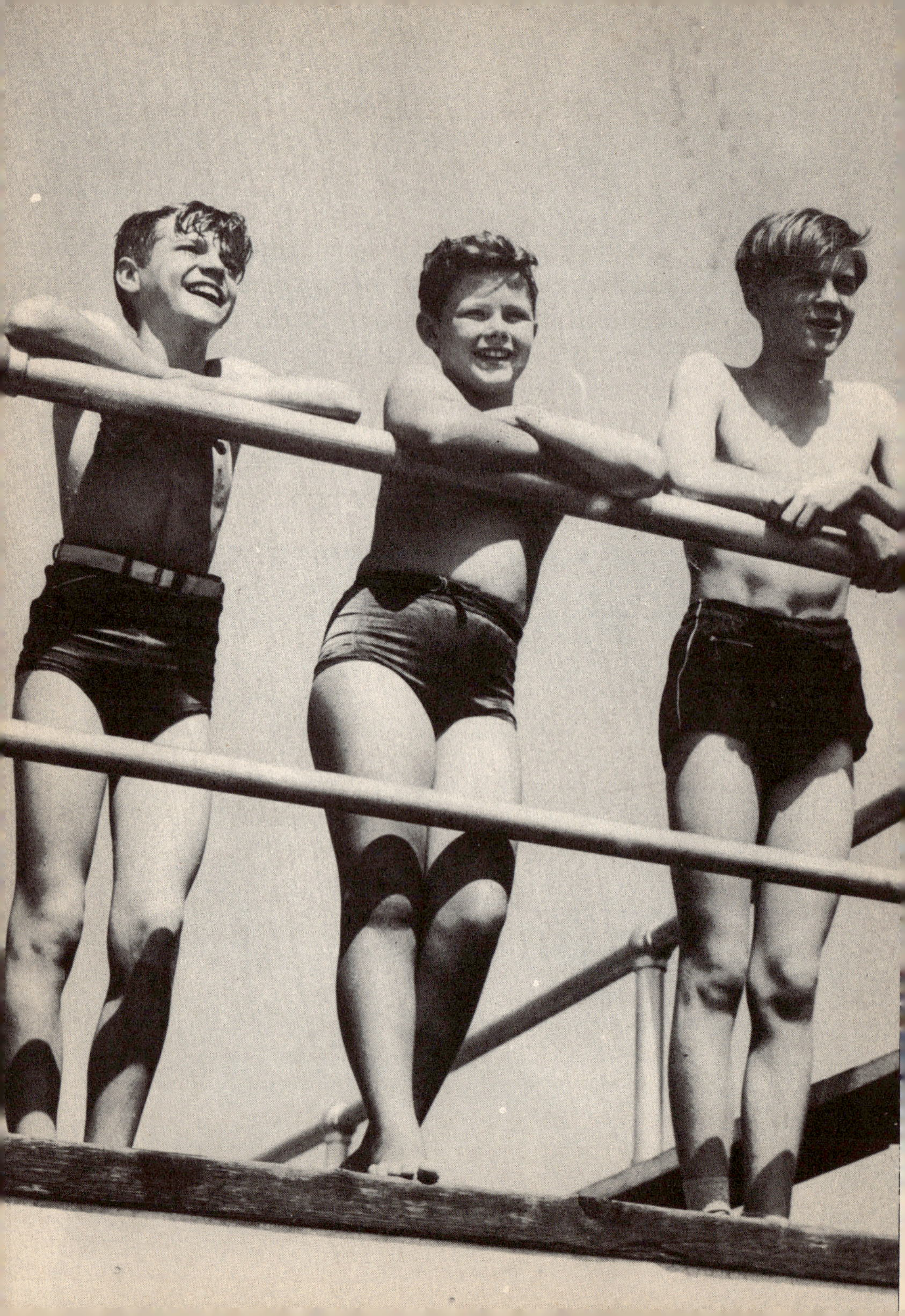

ACCIDENTS ON VACATION

SUNBURN

On the first swimming and tramping days of each year some people always get sunburned. They are not used to being out in the sun. None of us needs to have a sunburn if we take care to "warm up" little by little.

Right after school on warm days let the sun shine on your bare arms and neck for a few minutes. Go out in the sun on Saturdays and Sundays, too. Add a few minutes to your sunning each day. By summer vacation you will be ready for long hours of outdoor fun, without fear of sunburn.

People with very light hair and white skin can never safely let as much sun shine on their bare skin as darker people can. They must always be careful not to let the sun shine too long on their skin, no matter how carefully they may "work up" to prevent sunburn.

FISHHOOKS, GUNS, AND KNIVES

Fishhooks must be handled with the greatest care. Fishhooks caught in fingers often have to be cut out. The hook on the end of your line should be stuck in a cork or a small piece of wood when you are not fishing.

"Guns are always loaded," you should say to yourself every time you see a gun. When you are older, some grown person may show you how to use a gun. Until then leave all guns and pistols alone. Even BB guns are dangerous. They can cause blindness.

Knives are never playthings. They are tools, not toys. If you have a knife, always carry it closed or in a case hung from a belt. Learn how to use it as it should be used. Never let younger children touch it. A boy with a knife, like a man with a gun, must be very thoughtful of other people's safety. Look at page 219 again to see good form in using a knife and an ax.

THE CAMPFIRE

A campfire is a beautiful and exciting sight, but it can also be very dangerous. Do not build a campfire unless there is an older person with you. Learn how to put out a campfire with water, sand, or damp dirt. Never leave a campfire that is not entirely out. Be sure that the ashes are quite cold. A wind can make a forest fire from just one spark. Useful, beautiful trees are burned down and people often lose their lives in forest fires.

CAMP INJURIES

Injuries that often happen in camp and on tramping trips are cuts, sprains, bruises, burns, bumps from running into things or falling down, blisters on the feet, sore places caused by splinters, and even broken bones. If you are not sure what to do when you or someone with you has one of these injuries, review pages 189 to 196. When you are away on a camping trip, it is wise always to have a first-aid kit with you (a small box or bag of first-aid materials).

POISON IVY AND POISON * SUMAC

Even when we are out in the woods far away from the dangers of city streets, there are safety rules that we must remember.

Look at the picture below. The plant on the right has three leaves. It is a vine that you find growing

POISON SUMAC

POISON IVY

over stone walls, climbing trees, or even growing along the ground. You have heard its name. It is poison ivy.

Some people are badly poisoned by poison ivy. If they touch it, their skin becomes covered with a red rash and small white blisters which burn and itch. If you walk through poison ivy and get its oil on your shoes and stockings, you may get it on your hands and other parts of your body. The smoke from burning brush and poison ivy vines causes the most painful kind of ivy poisoning.

The Scouts are now using a method of treating poison ivy which is very successful. Find out about it.

The other plant shown on page 225 is poison sumac. Some people are badly poisoned by it. Sumac poisoning should be treated in the same way as ivy poisoning. (Both these plants are sometimes called poison oak.)

BOATING AND SWIMMING

Water accidents need not happen if we follow these rules:

1. Everyone should learn how to swim or at least to keep afloat. A person who has fallen into the water should "keep his head." He should lie flat on his back and flutter his hands. This is one way to keep afloat until help comes.

2. Everyone who goes swimming should take

time to see whether the swimming place is safe. A good swimming place

> (1) has no strong currents to pull one down or out into deep water;
> (2) is deep enough for those who want to dive;
> (3) has no rocks or sunken logs in it;
> (4) is free from disease germs.

3. Everyone should learn lifesaving. The Red Cross has a saying we should all remember. It is, "Row—throw—go—tow." If a person who cannot swim is in deep water, you can save him in these ways:

Row a boat out to him or push a log or a big board out to him.

Throw a rope or a life preserver to him.

Go to him if you can swim and have no boat with which you can reach him more quickly.

Tow him; that is, if you swam out to him, swim back to shore carrying him on your chest or back.

WHICH?

Which of these boys and girls were playing in the right way in the water? Give the reasons for your answers.

1. Bill had not yet learned to swim; so he did not go out in water over his head.
2. Alice could not swim, but she had water wings. With them she went out in the deep water.
3. David always had a swimming buddy when he went in swimming.
4. Dick did not want to be called a "fraid cat"; so he took dares to do dangerous stunts in the water.

5. Helen stayed in the water until her teeth began to chatter and she felt cold.

6. Although it was a very hot day, the Boy Scout troop waited for swimming until they found a pond where the water was clean and fresh.

7. Peter had fun calling, "Help, help," when he was out swimming in deep water. He laughed when someone came hurrying to rescue him.

8. When Jerry had learned to dive, he would dive into any lake or pool the minute he reached it.

9. At camp only the boys and girls who knew how to swim went out in the canoes.

10. Bob thought it was great fun to stand up in a rowboat and rock it.

11. When the wind was blowing very hard, Jack did not go out in his small boat.

12. Dorothy and Joan always chose their seats in a small boat before leaving shore. They kept those seats all the time they were on the water.

Things to Do

1. Be ready to tell in class what you should do
    (1) when you go out in a small boat.
    (2) when you want to dive in a spot where you have never been before.
    (3) when someone who is in a boat with you rocks the boat.
    (4) when you see children playing beside deep water.
    (5) when a friend wants you to go swimming right after you have eaten dinner.
2. Add to your list of habits the good habits you should practice when you are on or in the water.
3. Help someone you know learn how to swim.
4. Ask someone who has been to camp how water accidents are prevented there.

SAFE WATER BY THE WAY

Donald was on a hike with the Scouts. It was a very warm spring day. Everyone was perspiring. All the boys soon wanted a drink of water. Some of them had brought water with them. The others began to look for water.

"There is a clear, clean brook," said Donald. "I'll get a drink there." He got down on his knees and was about to drink when the Scout leader came up.

"Don't drink that water, Donald," he said. "It looks clear and it sparkles, but we do not know that it is safe. It may have bacteria in it that cause disease. It is better to be thirsty a little longer than to take a chance of getting sick."

So Donald walked on, more thirsty than ever. Soon they came to a pipe out of which some clear water was running. By the pipe was this sign: "City Water Supply—Safe Water for Drinking."

"There you are," said the leader. "Now you can have safe water to drink. Big cities are careful to have their water supply free from harmful bacteria. Drink slowly even though you are very thirsty."

WHICH ANSWERS ARE RIGHT?

Write your answers in your notebook or give them in class.

You can be sure water is safe to drink

(1) when it comes straight from the water supply of a large city.

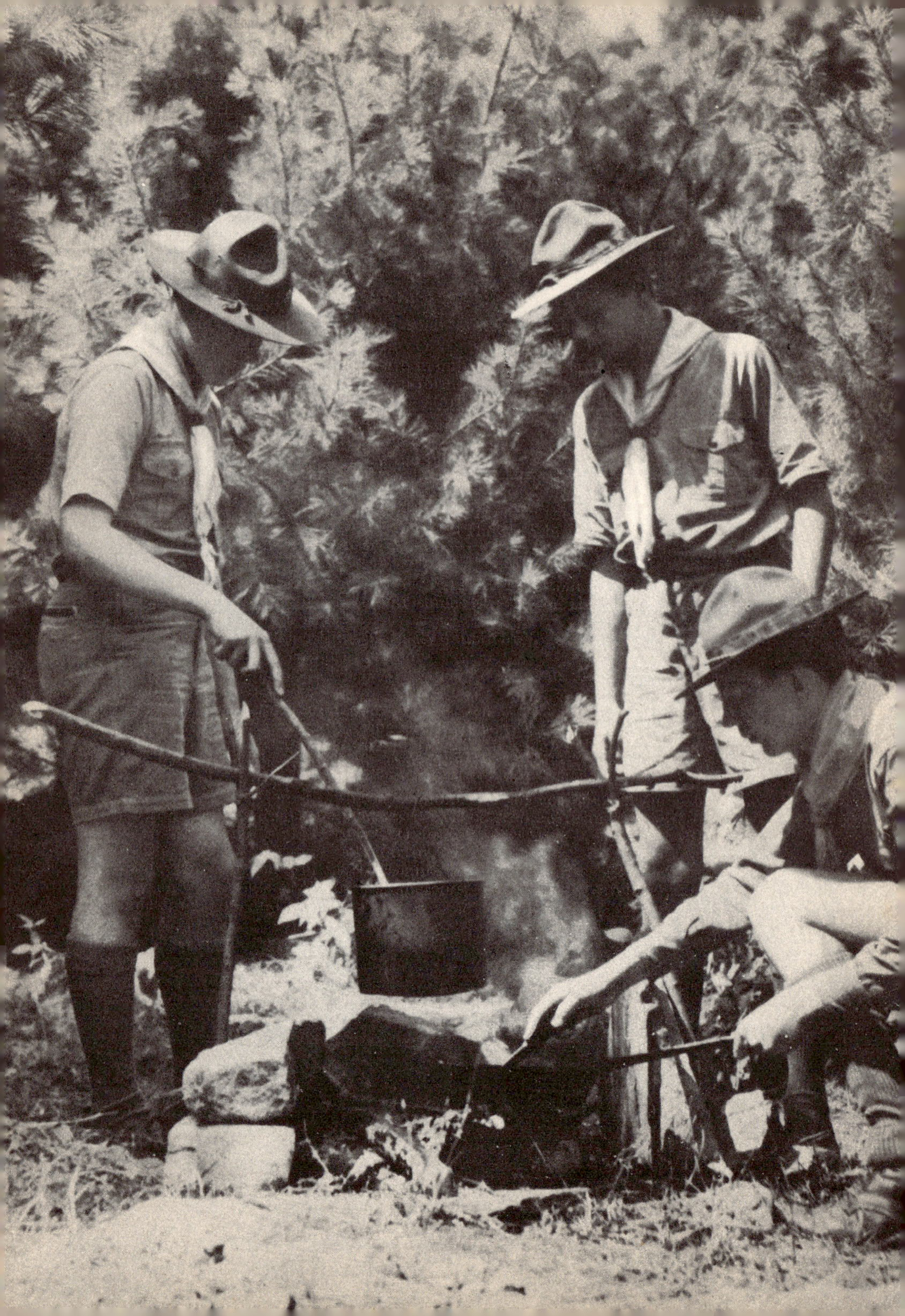

(2) when you have boiled it.
(3) when it looks clear and sparkling.
(4) when it comes from a brook.
(5) when it comes from an old well.
(6) when it bubbles up from a spring which is guarded carefully and kept clean.

Things to Do

1. Tell the class about the safe places where you get water when you go on a walk.

2. Read in a Scout book everything you can find about getting safe water on camping and walking trips. Also read about taking care of waste on a camping trip.

3. Keep your record of height and weight during the summer vacation. Read pages 78 to 80 to find out what you should do to gain in weight during the summer.

4. Write a story about a meal at camp. Tell in the story everything you can think of that would make mealtime at camp a happy time for everyone.

5. Have an exhibit of the best kinds of clothes to take to camp. You may use pictures if you wish to.

6. Find out what work the forest rangers in your state do.

7. Stop reading for a minute to look at the way you are sitting and holding your book. Then turn back to the section on posture to see whether you are following all the directions for good sitting posture. Also notice whether the light falls on your book from behind and above.

8. Look back over the pages in this unit and find the starred term. Add it to your dictionary. If you have done this for the starred words in each unit, you now have a list of many new words. Keep your dictionary so that you can add new words to it next year.

GLOSSARY

This glossary explains the hard words or expressions as they are used in this book. You will find in the glossary the words in the text that have a star (*) after them.

Key to Sounds

ā *as in* āte
â *as in* car′bon-âte
â *as in* câre
ă *as in* ăm
ă *as in* fi′năl
ä *as in* ärm
à *as in* àsk
à *as in* so′fà
ē *as in* ēve
ê *as in* ê-vent′
ĕ *as in* ĕnd
e *as in* move′mĕnt
ẽ *as in* moth′ẽr
ī *as in* īce
ĭ *as in* ĭll
ō *as in* ōld
ȯ *as in* ȯ-bey′
ô *as in* ôr′der
ŏ *as in* ŏdd
ỏ *as in* lỏss
ŏ *as in* cŏr-rect′
oi *as in* oil
o͞o *as in* fo͞od
o͝o *as in* fo͝ot
ou *as in* out
ū *as in* ūse
û *as in* û-nite′
û *as in* bûrn
ŭ *as in* ŭp
ŭ *as in* cir′cŭs
th *as in* bathe
zh *like the* s *in* treas′ure

ABDOMEN (ăb-dō′mĕn). The part of the body just below the chest which contains the stomach and bowels.

ACID (ăs′ĭd). Something that is sharp or biting to the taste.

ACUTE (à-kūt′). Sharp or severe, as the pain of a toothache.

ADENOID (ăd′ê-noid). A spongy growth or swelling that partly closes the pathway between the nose and throat.

ADENOID TISSUE (tĭsh′ū). *See* adenoid *and* tissue.

ADHESIVE TAPE (ăd-hē′sĭv tāp). A sticky tape used to hold a covering on a wound.

AIR SACS (âr săks). Tiny baglike pockets in the lungs which hold the air we breathe.

ALCOHOL (ăl′kȯ-hŏl). A liquid used on wounds to kill germs. The colorless liquid in beer, wine, and whisky which makes people drunk.

ALCOHOLIC (ăl′kȯ-hŏl′-ĭk). Containing some alcohol.

ARCH (ärch). A curve like that of a stone bridge.

BACTERIA (băk-tē′rĭ-a̦). Very small living things that belong to the plant kingdom. They are too small to be seen with the eyes alone. We call one of them a bacterium.

BAKING SODA (bāk′ĭng sō′da̦). A white powder used for burns and insect bites.

BANDAGE (băn′dĭj). A strip of cloth or other material used in dressing and binding up a cut or other wound or an injured leg or arm.

BLISTER (blĭs′tēr). A swelling of the skin filled with blood or white liquid from the blood.

BLOOD VESSEL (blŭd vĕs′'l). Tube in the body through which the blood flows.

BORIC ACID SOLUTION (bō′rĭk ăs′ĭd sȯ-lū′shŭn). An eyewash made by mixing a white powder with water. It is also used to wash cuts and other wounds.

BOWEL MOVEMENT (bou′ĕl mōōv′mĕnt). A way of getting rid of the waste material of the body.

BRAIN (brān). The part of the body within the skull, or head bones.

BRUISE (brōōz). To hurt or injure without breaking the skin. A cut is not a bruise.

BUNION (bŭn′yŭn). A red, sore swelling, usu-

233

ally on a joint of the big toe.

CARBON (kär′bŏn). The substance of which coal and charcoal are made. Mixed with other substances, carbon is found in most animals and plants.

CARBON DIOXIDE (kär′bŏn dī-ŏk′sīd). A gas having no color, no odor, no taste. Fire will not burn in it. Plants use it in making food.

CAVITY (kăv′ĭ-tĭ). A hole.

CHICKEN POX (chĭk′ĕn pŏks). A very catching disease, usually a children's disease.

CHLORINE (klō′rēn). A bad-smelling gas with a greenish yellow color. It is very irritating to the nose and throat.

CIRCULATE (sûr′kṷ-lāt). To move from the heart through the body and back to the heart. The blood circulates.

COD–LIVER OIL (kŏd-lĭv′ẽr oil). An oil from the liver of the codfish. People use it in the winter because it partly takes the place of sunshine.

COLD STORAGE (kōld stōr′ĭj). A way of keeping food cold so that it will not spoil.

COMMUNITY (kŏ-mū′-nĭ-tĭ). The place where a group of people live; a group of people living or working together.

CONTRACT (kŏn-trăkt′). To become smaller or shorter.

CORN (kôrn). A hard place in the skin with a tender, sore spot in the middle; usually found on a toe.

CORRECTIVE (kŏ-rĕk′-tĭv). Correcting or making better.

CROWN (kroun). The part of a tooth that shows above the gum.

CUSTARD (kŭs′tẽrd). A food made of eggs, milk, and sugar. It may be either boiled or baked.

DDT. A substance that kills flies, mosquitoes, and other insects.

DECAY (dĕ-kā′). The state of rotting; to rot.

DEFECT (dĕ-fĕkt′). A weakness or fault, as an eye defect.

DENTAL (dĕn′tăl). Having to do with the teeth or the work of the dentist.

DENTAL FLOSS (dĕn′-tăl flŏs). A kind of thread used to clean between the teeth.

DENTINE (dĕn′tēn). The hard, bony material beneath the enamel of the tooth. Most of the tooth is made of dentine.

DIET (dī′ĕt). The usual food of a person or an animal.

DIGESTION (dĭ-jĕs′-chŭn). The breaking of food into very small bits and changing into a liquid form so that it can be used by the body.

DIPHTHERIA (dĭf-thē′-rĭ-a̤). A dangerous disease affecting the throat.

DRAFT (dra̤ft). A current of air such as blows through a room when a window and a door are open at the same time.

DRUG (drŭg). Anything used as a medicine or in making medicines. Certain drugs are habit forming and very dangerous.

EARDRUM (ēr′drŭm′). A thin skinlike part of the ear that helps in hearing. It is stretched tight, across the opening, like the top of a drum.

ENAMEL (ĕn-ăm′ĕl). The hard, shiny, outside coat of a tooth, above the gum.

ENRICH (ĕn-rĭch′). To make food better by adding vitamins and sometimes other good things.

EXAMINATION (ĕg-zăm′ĭ-nā′shŭn). A test. A health examination is a testing of one's health.

EXHALE (ĕks-hāl′). To breathe air out of the lungs.

EXPERIMENT (ĕks-pĕr′ĭ-mĕnt). A kind of trial or test to find out the truth about something.

235

FATIGUE (fȧ-tēg′). A tired feeling.

FEVER (fē′vẽr). Body temperature that is higher than usual.

FIRST AID (fûrst ād). Treatment given, when no doctor is at hand, to people who have been hurt or become ill.

FLABBY (flăb′ĭ). Limp or weak.

GAUZE (gôz). Very thin cloth. White gauze is used on wounds.

GERMS (jûrmz). Small living things, some of which may cause certain kinds of sickness.

HABIT-FORMING (hăb′ĭt-fôrm′ĭng). Forming a habit which is hard to break.

HEALTH EXAMINATION (hĕlth ĕg-zăm′ĭ-nā′shŭn). *See* examination.

HEALTH OFFICER (hĕlth ŏf′ĭ-sẽr). A person who helps people in a community to have better health. He sees that those who have catching diseases stay at home and does many other more important things, such as teaching grownups, inspecting water, and seeing that restaurants are kept clean and serve good food.

HEART (härt). A hollow muscle about the size of the fist which sends blood through the body.

IMMUNITY (ĭ-mū′nĭ-tĭ). Resistance to disease or poison.

INHALE (ĭn-hāl′). To breathe air into the lungs.

INJURY (ĭn′jẽr-ĭ). A hurt of some kind.

IODINE (ī′ŏ-dīn). A substance often used in liquid form to kill germs on cuts and other injuries.

IRON (ī′ẽrn). A substance needed to make red blood. It is found in egg yolk, green leaves, and liver.

IRREGULAR (ĭr-rĕg′ŭ-lẽr). Not even.

IRRITATE (ĭr′ĭ-tāt). To stir up and make unpleasant.

ITCHING (ĭch′ĭng). Feeling so that one wants to scratch the skin.

JOINT (joint). The place at which two bones are joined.

JUNKET (jŭng′kĕt). A pudding made of milk and sugar.

LABORATORY (lăb′ȯ-rȧ-tō′rĭ). A place where scientific work is done.

LENGTHWISE ARCH (lĕngth′wīz ärch). In the foot it is an arch reaching from the heel to the toe.

LUNGS (lŭngz). The part of the body which fills with air when we breathe in.

MANURE (mȧ-nūr′). Wastes from horses and other animals.

MEASLES (mē′z′lz). A catching disease which causes the skin to break out with small, red spots and gives the person a fever.

MICROSCOPE (mī′krȯ-skōp). An instrument with a lens, or piece of glass, for making things look larger than they are.

MINERAL (mĭn′ẽr-ăl). A substance, like iron, which is found in foods and which is needed by the body.

MOLAR (mō′lẽr). One of the twelve back teeth, which grind the food.

MUMPS (mŭmps). A catching disease which causes fever and swelling in the neck and face.

MUSCLE (mŭs″l). The tissue in the bodies of animals and people which makes it possible for the body to move.

NECK (nĕk). The part of a tooth between the crown and the root.

NERVE (nûrv). One of the threadlike cords that carry messages back and forth in the body.

NERVOUS (nûr′vŭs). Having the nerves diseased or overexcited.

ORGAN (ôr′găn) Part of

237

an animal or a plant which does a certain thing for it. The eyes, the heart, and the stomach are organs of the body.

OXYGEN (ŏk'sĭ-jĕn). A gas that is part of the air we breathe. It is necessary to life. It has no color, odor, or taste.

PASTEURIZE (păs'tẽr-īz). To heat hot enough and long enough to kill most of the germs.

PATIENT (pā'shĕnt). A person who is being treated by a doctor.

PERSPIRE (pẽr-spīr'). To sweat.

PETROLEUM JELLY (pê-trō'lê-ŭm jĕl'ĭ). A jellylike substance used in first aid.

POISON IVY (poi'z'n ī'vĭ). A plant poisonous to many people.

POISON SUMAC (poi'-z'n sū'măk). A bush having poisonous leaves and stems.

POLLEN (pŏl'ĕn). The fine powder on some flowers and grasses.

POSTURE (pŏs'tŭr). The position of the body.

PROTECTIVE (prō-tĕk'-tĭv). Protecting; preventing injury.

RASH (răsh). A reddening or breaking out of small red spots on the skin.

RELAX (rĕ-lăks'). To loosen up, become less stiff.

RESIST (rĕ-zĭst'). To act against; to keep from getting a disease.

RESISTANCE (rĕ-zĭs'-tăns). Resisting something; the ability of the body to fight against germs.

RHEUMATIC FEVER (roo-măt'ĭk fē'vẽr). A serious disease, usually in children and young people. There are fever and pain around the joints. It sometimes harms the heart.

ROOT (root). The part of a tooth below the gum.

SCARLET FEVER (skär'lĕt fē'vẽr). A serious catching disease that causes a bright red rash, sore throat, and fever.

SCHEDULE (skĕd'ūl). A plan or record for spending time.

SCHICK TEST (shĭk tĕst). A test to see if one is likely to catch diphtheria.

SCIENTIST (sī'ĕn-tĭst). A person who knows much about science.

SEVERE (sė-vēr'). Sharp or violent; serious.

SMALLPOX (smôl'pŏks'). A disease which often leaves ugly marks on the skin.

SPINAL COLUMN (spī'năl kŏl'ŭm). The spine, or backbone.

SPLINT (splĭnt). Thin strip of wood for holding a broken bone in place.

SPRAIN (sprān). To injure a joint by a sudden twist.

STERILE (stĕr'ĭl). Free from germs.

STIMULANT (stĭm'ŭ-lănt). Something that stirs a person up, excites him. A stimulant may make the heart beat faster than usual.

STRAIN (strān). Injury by too much effort or by stretching.

TEMPERATURE (tĕm'-pẽr-à-tŭr). Degree of heat or cold.

TENDON (tĕn'dŭn). A strong cord joining a muscle to a bone.

TETANUS (tĕt'à-nŭs). A serious disease caused by certain bacteria, usually in wounds.

THERMOMETER (thẽr-mŏm'ė-tẽr). An instrument for measuring temperature.

THERMOS BOTTLE (thûr'mŏs bŏt''l). A bottle for keeping food at a certain temperature. It keeps hot food hot and cold food cold.

TISSUE (tĭsh'ū). A substance forming the parts of animals and plants, such as skin tissue or bone tissue.

TONSIL (tŏn'sĭl). Small oval mass at the back of the mouth.

TOXOID (tŏk'soid). A

239

kind of medicine used to keep a person from catching diphtheria and certain other diseases.

TUBERCULOSIS (tū-bûr′kŭ-lō′sĭs). A disease caused by a certain kind of bacterium, which often attacks the lungs.

TYPHOID FEVER (tī′-foid fē′vẽr). A very dangerous disease caused by germs taken into the body, often in food or drink.

VACCINATE (văk′sĭ-nāt). To protect by vaccine against smallpox.

VACCINATION (văk′sĭ-nā′shŭn). Having a doctor put vaccine against smallpox into the skin.

VACCINE (văk′sēn). The germs of a disease weakened or killed and used to protect people against that disease.

VIRUS (vī′rŭs). A very small germ found growing in a person or in an animal suffering from any one of certain kinds of diseases.

VITAMIN (vī′tȧ-mĭn). A special substance necessary in the proper food, found especially in milk, butter, raw fruits and vegetables, and cod-liver oil.

WATER GLASS (wô′tẽr glȧs). A liquid in which eggs can be kept to prevent spoiling.

WHOOPING COUGH (hōōp′ĭng kŏf). A disease, usually caught by children, which causes a great deal of hard coughing. It is catching.

WINDPIPE (wĭnd′pīp). The passage from the throat to the lungs.

X–RAY (ĕks′rā). To examine or take pictures, as of the lungs, with X rays. X rays can pass through many substances that light rays cannot pass through.

INDEX

abdomen, 91, 115
acids, 53, 97
adenoids, 9, 88, 89, 100
adhesive tape, 130, 189, 193
air, 9-10, 69, 88-90, 148
alcohol for injuries, 130, 181, 189, 190, 192, 193
alcoholic drinks, 131-133, 197
animals, 17-24, 32-34, 67, 139; overcoming fear of, 27, 32-34; safety with, 33, 204
appearance, healthy, 73
appetite, 143
apples, 22, 78, 98, 137, 141, 153-158
arithmetic, improving in, 36-38
asparagus, 82
axes, 218

backbone, 117-118
bacon, 155-156
bacteria, 179; and flies, 148, 166, 179; immunity to, 103-109; in milk, 147-149; in teeth, 97; in water, 105, 229; spread of, 4-7, 8, 9, 12, 13, 89, 107, 183. *See also* germs
baking soda, 189, 192, 193
bandage, sterile, 130, 181, 189
baseball safety, 206
baths, 10; animal, 18-19
bed, 8, 59
bedtime, 12, 21, 49-50, 57, 58-60
bee stings, 193
beef, 33, 156
beets, 140, 144, 150
bicycle safety, 21, 202

birds, 167
blisters, 130, 181, 193, 212, 224
blood, 67-69, 90-91, 117, 144; vessels, 90, 96, 118-119
boating, safe, 226-227
bones, 117-118, 150; broken, 195, 201, 210-211, 224
books, clean, 174, 182
boric acid solution, 189, 192
bowel movement, 12, 117
brain, 86
bread, for animals, 33, 76-77; for health and growth, 70, 76-77, 78, 80; for teeth, 98; in meals, 22, 153-158; in sickness, 10, 13
breathing, 10, 130
brown Betty, 156
bruises, 192, 224
bunions, 122
burns, 190-191, 212-216, 224
burros, 17-24
buses, safety on, 198-199
butter, 13, 22, 75, 78, 80, 153-158

cabbage, 98, 141, 153-156
cake, 42, 80
camp life, 25-30, 49-52, 66
camping, safe, 223-231
candy, 80
carbon, 146
carbon dioxide, 67-69, 146
carrots, 75, 82, 98, 137, 140, 141, 144, 150, 156
cats, 204
cauliflower, 82
celery, 22, 98

241

cereal, 12, 33, 70, 78, 153
character development, 15-46
cheeks, 21
chicken pox, 14, 109
chickens, 18, 75, 135, 144
chipmunks, 197
chlorine, 105
chocolate, 172
churches, 159, 174-175
cinnamon, 156
citizenship, 162, 178
clothes, 9
cocoa, 78
cod-liver oil, 10
coffee, 61, 133
cold storage, 144
colds, 3-13, 57, 86-87, 107, 179
community, 159; and health, 179-185; helping your, 161-168; Indian, 161; knowing your, 170-175; school, 175-176; spirit, 168-170
cookies, 158
corns, 122-123
cotton, sterile, 189, 190
coughing, 7, 13, 148, 179
country roads, safety on, 197
cows, 135, 147
cream, 78. *See also* milk
crown of tooth, 96
custard, 3, 13
cuts, 181, 224

dark, overcoming fear of, 30-32
DDT, 167
deafness, 87, 107
decay, tooth, 95-100
defects, body, 77, 83, 84
dental floss, 98

dentine, 96, 97, 100
dentist, 87, 95-100
dictionary, health, 14
digestion, 117
diphtheria, 103, 104, 106, 159, 179
dirt, 103, 147
diseases, catching, 4-7, 57; preventing, 7-9, 73-92, 103-110, 179, 182; taking care of, 1, 8-13, 107-108
doctor, 195
dogs, 32-34, 204
draft, 9
drowning, saving from, 227
drugs, habit-forming, 132-133
dust, 10, 89, 147
dusting, 184

eardrum, 86, 87
ears, 83-84, 86-87
eggs, 70, 75, 78, 135, 144, 154-158
electricity, safety with, 216
enamel of tooth, 96, 97, 98
examinations, health. *See* tests
exercise, 9, 84-85; and rest, 53-56; for feet, 127, 129; for health and growth, 77, 78; hiking, 54-55, 66, 170-173; need of muscles for, 64-66
experiment, oxygen, 66-67; sleep, 57; with plants, 145-146; with rats, 75-77
eye dropper, 189, 192
eyes, 21, 56, 64, 78, 109, 119, 163, 192; care of, 84-85

falls, 192, 194-195, 201, 202, 209-212

fatigue, 12, 118
fear, overcoming, of animals, 27, 32-34; of dark, 30-32; of water, 25-30
feet, 121-130
fever, 3, 8, 108
fire, and germs, 8, 184; camp-, 49, 224; need of oxygen for, 66-67; safety, 215-216, 224
first aid, 187-196
fish, 70, 158
fishhooks, 223
fish-liver oil, 10, 33, 98
flatfoot, 126
flies, 20, 103, 148, 165-167, 179, 192
food, 135; and bacteria, 7, 166; and blood, 91; and colds, 3, 8, 10, 12, 13; and feet, 127; and muscles, 70; and posture, 117; and teeth, 96, 98; for animals, 18-23, 33; for health and growth, 75-77, 78, 91, 150; fresh vegetables, 137-144; in good meals, 152-158; minerals and vitamins in, 144, 149-151; safe, 180; safe milk, 104, 147-149, 166; test with rats, 75-77
footprints, 123-127
friends, 15-46
fruit, 21, 135; and colds, 3, 7, 8, 10, 12, 13; and muscles, 70; and teeth, 98; for health and growth, 75, 78, 80, 91; in good meals, 153-158; vitamins in, 150

garbage, 161, 162, 165, 168
gardens, 137-144

gas, safety with, 214, 216
gauze, sterile, 181, 189, 190, 191, 193
germs, 103, 179-184; and flies, 148, 166, 179; from animals, 204; immunity to, 103-109; in adenoids and tonsils, 9, 89; in ears, 86; in injuries, 105, 190, 193, 212; in milk, 147-149; in teeth, 97; in water, 105, 229; spread of, 4-7, 8, 9, 12, 13, 89, 107, 183
grain, 95
grapefruit, 158
grass, 17, 19, 20, 75, 164
growth, of animals, 22-24, 33; of good character traits, 15-46; of people, 17, 23-24, 56-58, 91, 133; tests, 75-83. *See also* food
gums, 96, 98
guns, 223-224

habits, 7-12, 83, 91
hair, animal, 19, 76
handkerchiefs, 5, 7, 8, 13, 179
hands, washing, 8, 13, 180, 182, 185
hay fever, 163-165
headache, 4, 109
health officers, 162
heart, 57, 83, 90-91, 107, 117, 131
height, 17, 24, 81, 84
hiking, 54-55, 66, 170-173
home safety, 208-220

ice, ashes for, 169
icebox, 147
immunity, 103-109, 165

243

Indian walk, 111, 123-124
insects, 167
iodine, 130, 189, 193
iron in food, 144, 145
ivy, poison, 192-193, 225-226

jaws, 64, 100
joints, 63, 89
junket, 3, 13

kerosene and fire, 216
kittens, 75
knives, 190, 218, 223-224
kola nut, 61

laboratory, 75
lettuce, 98, 140, 141, 144
libraries, 44, 173-174, 175
lifesaving, 227
light, 30-32, 84, 145-146
lockjaw, 103, 106
lungs, 67, 83, 87-90, 117, 144

manure, 140, 165
matches, safety with, 215, 218
meals, 22, 78, 142, 152-158
measles, 14, 91, 106, 107, 179
meat, 13, 33, 70, 75
mental health, 15-46
microscope, 4
milk, 21; and colds, 3, 13; and muscles, 70; and teeth, 98; for animals, 22, 33; for health and growth, 75-77, 78, 133; in good meals, 22, 142, 152-158; minerals and vitamins in, 149, 151; safe, 104, 147-149, 166
minerals in food, 144, 149-151
mistakes, 35-41
mouth, 8, 179-183

mumps, 14
muscles, and posture, 115-118; and rest, 52-56, 78; as health sign, 21; in feet, 125; needs of, 64-70; of eyes, 84; work of, 62-64

nature walk, 170-173
neck of tooth, 96
needles, 189, 193, 218
nerves, 86, 96, 100, 131
nose, 4, 7, 9, 10, 67, 83, 86, 87-90, 109, 163
nosebleed, 190, 201

oak, poison, 226
oatmeal, 153-157
oats for animals, 18, 23
oil and fire, 216
onions, 140, 141, 144, 155-156
orange juice, 3, 42-43, 78, 98
oranges, 78, 117, 172
organs of body, 57, 116
oxygen, for muscles, 66-67, 117; for plants, 145, 146; in blood, 91, 144

parks, 168-170
peas, 82, 140, 141, 144
personality development, 15-46
perspiration, 9
petroleum jelly, 189, 190
picnic grounds, 168-169
pigweed, 165
plants, 67, 75, 145-146
play, day, 43-45; for health and growth, 78, 91; safety, 201-206; time for, 51-52
poison ivy, 192-193, 225-226
poison oak, 226
poison sumac, 226

244

pollen, 163
posture, 17, 21, 73, 83, 91, 111, 113-121
potatoes, 3, 13, 82, 137, 144, 153-158
pueblos, 161
pumpkins, 140, 142, 144

quarrels, preventing, 38-40

rabbits, 75
radishes, 140, 141, 144
ragweed, 162-165
railroads, safety in crossing, 199
raisins, 22, 156
rash, 107, 109, 193
rats, food test with, 75-77
reading, 36-37, 173-174
refrigerator, 147
relaxing, 60-61, 78
rest, and colds and other diseases, 3, 8, 12; and eyes, 84-85; and feet, 127; and muscles, 52-56; for health and growth, 21, 78
rheumatic fever, 89-90
root of tooth, 96
rubbish, 161-162, 168, 169, 170, 185, 217-218
Russian thistle, 165

safety, 57, 175; at railroad crossings, 199; for ears, 87; in outdoor play, 201-206; in school, 206-208; on street and road, 35, 196-198; on streetcars and buses, 198-199; to prevent burns, 212-216; to prevent falling, 209-212; to prevent other accidents, 216-218; vacation, 223-229

sagebrush, 165
salads, 22, 141, 156
sandwiches, 21, 172
saving, money, 131, 152-156; time, 49-52
scarlet fever, 3, 14, 91, 106, 107-108, 179
schedule for day, 12, 13, 51-54
Schick test, 104
school, clean, 182; community spirit in, 175-176; doctor, 83-91, 93, 108-109; nurse, 83-91, 93, 107-109, 152; posture in, 118-120; safety in, 206-208
scissors, 218
Scouts, 170-173, 175, 229
scratches, 181
screens, 166-167
sharp things, safety with, 87, 203-204, 205, 218
shoes, 9, 121-130
skin, 10, 21, 181
sleep, 21, 133; and colds, 12; for health and growth, 17, 56-58, 77, 78; rules for, 60-61
smallpox, 103-104, 106
smoke in air, 10
smoking, 130-131
sneezing, 5, 7, 8, 13, 148, 165, 179, 182
soap, 180, 192
soil, 139, 146
soup, 3, 13, 140, 141, 144, 156
spinach, 3, 82, 140
spinal column, 117-118
splinters in skin, 193, 224
splints, 195
sprains, 194-195, 224
squirrels, 197
stairs, safety for, 209, 210, 211

245

stew, 156
stimulants, 61
stockings, 121, 123, 129
stoves, 213-215
strain, 115, 118
street, safety on the, 196-197
streetcar safety, 198-199
sumac, poison, 226
sunburn, 223
sunshine, 9, 14, 77, 78, 98, 184, 185, 223
sweeping, 183-184
sweets, 10
swimming, 25-30, 226-227
Swiss chard, 140, 144

tea, 61, 133
teeth, 83, 87, 93-102, 150, 203
temperature, for eggs, 144; for plants, 145, 146; of body, 10, 108; of room, 10, 14
tendons, 63-64
tests, health, 9, 73-92, 97-99
tetanus, 103, 106
thermometer, 14
thermos bottle, 172
throat, 9, 10, 67, 83, 86, 87-90, 109; and smoking, 131
time, saving, 12, 13, 49-52
toes, 122
tomato juice, 78, 98, 137
tomatoes, 78, 137, 139, 140, 141, 142, 144, 155-156
tonsils, 9, 89
toothbrush, 98, 180
towels, 8, 13, 85, 182
toxoid, 104
training rules, 130-134
trees, climbing, 204
tuberculosis, 106

typhoid fever, 103, 104-105, 106, 179

vacations, safe, 25, 223-231
vaccination, 103-104
vaccine, 104-105
vaseline, 189, 190
vegetables, 175; and colds, 3, 10, 12, 13; and muscles, 70; and teeth, 98; book of, 82-83; for health and growth, 75, 78, 91; fresh, 137-144; in good meals, 153-158; minerals and vitamins in, 150
viruses, 4-7, 9, 12, 163, 179
vitamins, 10, 98, 149-151, 158

"warming up," 65-66
washcloths, 85
washing hands and face, 8, 13, 180, 182, 185
waste products of body, 91
water, and colds, 3, 8, 10, 12, 13; and fire, 215-216; and germs, 4; for animals, 18, 23, 33; for plants, 145, 146; overcoming fear of, 25-30; safe, 104-105, 162, 180, 226-227, 229-231
water glass, 144-145
weeds, 141
weight, 17, 21, 75-77, 81, 84; rules for gaining, 78-80
whooping cough, 103, 105-106
windows, open, 69-70
windpipe, 67-69, 89
work, 52-53
wormweed, 165

X ray, 90, 106

246